PANTHER BABY

Panther Baby

A Life of Rebellion and Reinvention

by Jamal Joseph DISCARD

ALGONQUIN BOOKS OF CHAPEL HILL   2012

Published by
Algonquin Books of Chapel Hill
Post Office Box 2225
Chapel Hill, North Carolina 27515-2225

a division of
Workman Publishing
225 Varick Street
New York, New York 10014

Library of Congress Cataloging-in-Publication Data
  Joseph, Jamal.
    Panther baby : a life of rebellion and reinvention /
by Jamal Joseph. — 1st ed.
        p. cm.
    "Published simultaneously in Canada
by Thomas Allen & Son Limited" — T.p. verso.
    ISBN 978-1-56512-950-4 (HC)
    ISBN 978-1-61620-129-6 (PB)
    1. Joseph, Jamal. 2. Joseph, Jamal — Childhood and youth.
3. Joseph, Jamal — Imprisonment. 4. Black Panther Party —
Biography. 5. African Americans — Biography. 6. African American
young men — New York (State) — New York — Biography. 7. Bronx
(New York, N.Y.) — Race relations — History — 20th century. 8. New
York (N.Y.) — Race relations — History — 20th century. 9. Bronx (New
York, N.Y.) — Biography. 10. New York (N.Y.) — Biography. I. Title.
    E185.97 J787A3 2011
    974.7'1043092 — dc23
    [B]   2011032139

10 9 8 7 6 5 4 3 2 1
First Edition

PANTHER BABY

1

The Path to Manhood

Good. Now do it blindfolded."

I looked down at the gleaming M16 assault rifle I was holding and then up at the three Black Panther officers standing over me. I was fifteen years old, sitting in the middle of the floor in a Panther safe house. A .45-caliber pistol, a 12-gauge shotgun and an M1 carbine were laid out in front of me. My mouth was dry, and nervous sweat ran down my back. The Panthers had told me that my life and the life of my fellow Panthers were on the line. Error equals death. I looked up at Yedwa, my weapons instructor, and I spaced out. He had a shoulder holster with a .357 Magnum, a black beret, goatee, muscular physique, and a mad gleam in his eye that denoted he was a crazy brother, more commonly known as a crazy nigger (a wild-assed black man who would say anything, do anything, and who courted death with a smile).

The ghetto had a ranking system when it came to manhood. You could be a punk, hard, bad, or crazy. Being a soft dude meant that you were a goody-goody who was scared to fight. Punk dudes got no respect and often got their "ass shook and their lunch money took." Hard dudes were fighters, but not like bad niggers, who would be swinging, cutting, and shooting while the hard dudes would be in heightened stages of argument. The bad niggers got all the respect. But to truly be a legend, you had to be a crazy nigger, meaning you had to give up on the possibility of a normal future and accept that any moment, any place, was a good time to die.

This manhood ranking system was connected to the idea of protecting your property, which was referred to as "mine" or "yours" as in, "I've got to protect mine" or "You gotta get yours." This was part of the code of honor we learned from the older guys. Since we were all poor, "mine" or "yours" didn't mean real estate, bank accounts, or stocks. It was more like a bike, sneakers, a girl, your mother's honor, or a couple of square feet on a street corner. What you claimed and how far you would go to protect "mine" or "yours" determined your manhood ranking.

In 1968 nobody was badder than the Panthers. They took the manhood rating to another level. Not only were they willing to fight and die for "theirs," they were also willing to lay down their lives for every man, woman, and child in the black community whether they knew them personally or not. Plus there were no boundaries to their craziness. They were willing to take on the police, the army, the government, every-damn-body.

And here I was, an orphan, a church boy, and an honor student with an M16 on my lap, pursuing the path to manhood.

"Brother, did you hear me?" Yedwa barked. "I said do it blindfolded."

I snapped out of my daze, pulled a bandanna out of my jean pocket, and tied it around my eyes. Katara, an eighteen-year-old Panther, helped me adjust the blindfold so I couldn't see. Then I began to disassemble the M16 by touch, laying the pieces in a line so I could grope for them when it was time to put the rifle back together.

I could hear Yedwa's voice through my personal darkness. "If the pigs attack at night, they ain't waitin' for you to turn on a light to get your shit together. In fact, if you turn on a light, they're going to use it to lock and unload on your ass."

"Right on, brother," said another Panther voice. I dropped the gun bolt on the floor. It clattered loudly.

"Concentrate, young brother," Yedwa ordered. "Concentrate."

Five minutes later I had put the M16 back together. I pulled the bandanna from my eyes. It was soaked with sweat. Yedwa took the rifle from me and with the precision of a combat veteran ejected the clip, cleared the chamber, and checked the weapon. Then he passed it around to the other Panthers. Finally he motioned for me to stand. "You took four minutes and thirty seconds. That means your ass would have been dead three and a half minutes ago. Practice so you can get your speed up." With that he turned and put the rifle and the other weapons in a duffel bag. Then he put the duffel bag in a closet.

Katara put a bucket of Kentucky Fried Chicken and a bottle of wine on the coffee table. Yedwa put a John Coltrane album on the stereo. Sadik, the other Panther, grabbed one of the large pillows near the window and pulled it over to the table. I sat on the couch next to Yedwa. We all grabbed some chicken and started greasin' and sippin' wine from paper cups. The brothers talked about jazz, revolutionary lovemaking (that's where the man and woman scream, "Power to the people" instead of "Give it to me"), and bourgeois Negroes who have to be "offed" before the revolution comes.

Mainly, I listened. I had only been a Panther for about three months and I hadn't really found my place or my groove yet. Besides, I didn't want to say the wrong thing or make the wrong joke and be thought of as a counterrevolutionary. That was far worse than being called a punk, and I heard that the consequences were much more severe. It was safer to eat my chicken and nod my head profoundly, as if I were "a deep brother."

Sadik asked if we were off duty. Yedwa answered, "Yeah," and headed into the bedroom.

Sadik smiled and said, "Well, it's time to talk to Brother Roogie." That was his code name for reefer. He produced a joint and lit it, then passed it to me. I took a hit and started coughing my lungs out.

Yedwa came back in the room and took the joint away. "Watch it, brother," he said. "In fact, you shouldn't even be doing that shit. What are you, fifteen?"

"Sixteen and a half," I lied, trying to keep a straight face. By then I was floating, buzzed from the weed.

Yedwa turned on the black-and-white TV and adjusted the rabbit ears. The wine and the weed had my head feeling light, and my attention drifted from the conversation to the TV and to the posters of Che Guevara, Malcolm X, and Eldridge Cleaver that were taped to the wall. Che's eyes seemed to be looking right at me, following me as I reached for another piece of chicken. Was he trying to send me a secret revolutionary message from the beyond? I tried to play it cool as I shifted positions to see if Che was still checking me out. He was.

Suddenly Yedwa began cursing out the television. Richard Nixon was on the screen talking about the war in Vietnam.

"Quit oinking," Yedwa shouted. "You're a lying fucking pig."

The rest of us started laughing, but Yedwa was incensed.

He reached under the cushion of the couch, pulled out a .38, aimed at the television, and pulled the trigger. The shot sounded like a large gun cap, not like the boom you hear in the movies. My ears started ringing as I stared at the gaping hole in the Zenith picture tube.

"Damn, Yedwa. You blasted the tube," Sadik observed as he jumped to his feet.

"Motherfucking propaganda box," Yedwa replied with a snarl that turned into a laugh. We all started to laugh until Sadik saw a flashing light pass by the window of the third-floor apartment.

"The pigs!" he yelled as he double-checked by peeking through the curtain.

"Must have heard the shot," Katara said.

Yedwa retrieved the duffel bag and passed out the weapons.

I wound up with the same M16 I had been trained with. We tipped over the couch. Yedwa motioned for Katara and me to duck behind it and to take aim at the front door. Yedwa and Sadik took up posts by the front window. No one talked. The only sounds were John Coltrane's sax and our hearts pounding at the anticipation of the police raid. Stress flared in my body. I wondered what it would be like to take a life, how it would feel to have bullets rip through my body. My stomach pitched like it was being brushed from the inside with the hot, molten wings of butterflies flapping. My bowels churned like I was going to shit in my pants. But I couldn't go out like that, not in front of these brothers. I took a deep breath to calm myself and looked over at Che. He was looking at the door too.

All right then, this was it. I would go out like a revolutionary, surrounded by chicken bones, a wounded TV, and a possessed poster of Che. I gripped the M16 tighter and waited for a battering ram or a tank to blow the door off the hinges. Then there were footsteps, a pause, and the jingling of keys as someone entered the next apartment. Time passed. Three minutes. Ten? Finally Yedwa turned from the window. "They split," he said, "Guess they were messing with someone in another building." We tried to act cocky as we put the apartment back together, but I wondered if everyone was secretly as glad as I was that we didn't have to shoot it out.

Yedwa came over and patted me on the back. "You moved like you were ready, young brother," he said, smiling. "You got a lotta heart."

I beamed for a moment, then pulled my revolutionary composure together. "Thank you, brother," I replied, trying to drop my adolescent voice an octave. But I did feel good inside. I had been near battle and I had made a good impression on a Panther officer, the crazy nigger Yedwa. His hand on my shoulder felt like the wing of an eagle about to guide his favorite offspring into flight. Yedwa invited me to sit for some more wine and a store-bought apple pie. I nodded my thanks but instead reached for my coat, saying I had to check on Noonie, my adoptive grandmother. The truth was I was dangerously close to pushing my eight o'clock curfew. It was, after all, a school night.

2

Skin Color

The nature and nurture of my background and upbringing made me a skinny, curly-headed lightning rod for the storm of social change that was sweeping America. I was conceived in Cuba, most probably in Havana, where my parents were graduate students at the university. Before my mother could break the news that she was pregnant, my father had disappeared to fight alongside Fidel and Che in the revolution. My maternal grandparents sent my mother, Gladys, to New

York to have her baby. Gladys lived in Queens with a strict, overbearing aunt. She moved out of her aunt's apartment and placed me in foster care when I was seventeen days old.

In Cuba Gladys had been a debutante whose father, Alfred, had been a successful engineer originally from the island of Dominica. She grew up speaking Spanish and French in a big airy house in Santa Clara. Her major in graduate school was biology, with the dream of becoming a doctor or researcher, but in New York, in 1952, she was an unwed black Latina woman who couldn't speak English. Too proud and perhaps too angry to ask her father for help, she decided to place me in "temporary care" while she learned English, went back to college, and made a life for herself.

I was first raised by Alexander and Anna Jackson, a retired black couple who took foster kids into their Bronx home. Gladys found the couple through an ad in a local newspaper. Noonie Baltimore, a petite yet strong elderly black woman, came to the Jackson home as a housekeeper when I was four. When the Jacksons became ill, Noonie and her husband, Charles, became my "adopted" grandparents.

Gladys would send me money every month and visit me several times a year. She had gotten married and had two other children: my younger sister, Elba, and my baby brother, Luis. Her mother, Erundina, affectionately known as Alita, had come from Cuba to help take care of the children while Gladys worked and took college courses. There was sometimes talk of me going to Brooklyn to live with Gladys, but it never happened. She passed away during childbirth when I was ten.

By the time I came into their lives, Noonie was in her sixties and Charles "Pa" Baltimore was in his seventies. Their income consisted of Social Security and the few extra dollars Pa made taking numbers bets and Noonie made from working as a housekeeper for families in our black working-class Bronx neighborhood. They both had grown up in the South. Their parents and older siblings had been slaves. I grew up hearing firsthand stories about segregation, the Ku Klux Klan, burning crosses, beatings, and lynchings.

Pa Baltimore disliked and distrusted white people, calling them "crackers" and "redneck bastards." Noonie was a devout Christian who went to church and prayer meetings several times a week. She had strong reservations about white people but had met some "good ones" in the years that she worked as a domestic for wealthy white families. Still, white people were to be dealt with cautiously.

Noonie and Pa had both been members of Marcus Garvey's Back to Africa movement. They told stories of the grand parades led by Garvey and thousands of his followers through Harlem in the 1920s. Pa always talked about crackers framing and deporting Marcus Garvey because of his beliefs. "Crackers hate a black man who stands up," Pa would say. He would also refer to black people as Africans, at a time when most people used the terms "colored" and "Negro" to describe the race.

My neighborhood in the North Bronx comprised modest private homes and the Edenwald housing project. It was populated by black and Latino people up from the South and up from Harlem. This is where people with civil service or skilled labor jobs came when they had enough money to be one rung away from the ghetto but not quite enough to make it all the way to the suburbs.

The Edenwald project was a mix of working families and people on public assistance. The neighborhood had been Irish and Italian working class until Negroes started moving in during the 1950s. The whites who could afford to move away did, while the others held fast to certain blocks and avenues that gave the community an "up south" segregated feeling. Black kids didn't play on white blocks; white teens didn't walk through the projects. Maybe we weren't being fire-hosed, clubbed, and bitten by German shepherds like the Negroes in the South we saw on TV, but white storekeepers would kick us out, white teenagers would jump us, and white cops would beat the shit out of us for being in the wrong place at the wrong time.

"If you're black, get back." These were the words to a song that Pa Baltimore had in his old record collection. He played it for me and told me that this song had been a big hit in America in the 1940s. He made it clear that he didn't really like the song but played it every now and then to remind himself of how crackers felt about colored folks.

Pa Baltimore would sit in the living room and cuss out our old console model black-and-white TV. He could cuss at the TV all day, calling a young Harry Reasoner names like "a lying, onion-head motherfucking cracker." Noonie would walk into the living room and get on him for cussing in front of me. He would apologize and a few minutes later cuss the TV out again when Tarzan came on, "How the fuck a skinny-assed little peckerwood gonna fall out a god damned plane and tell the Africans, the lions, and the tigers what to do?" Pa Baltimore's swordlike tongue would also cut the other way when it came to black people. "Niggers are like crabs in a fucking basket. Soon as one tries to climb out, another one pulls their black ass down."

I loved Pa Baltimore. Sometimes his comments would annoy me if there was a TV show I really wanted to watch. But most of the time he was more entertaining than the show we were watching. Besides giving me great cuss phrases I could use on my friends, such as "limp dick, rooty poot, son of a bitch," he would help me with my homework, overpay me for running errands, and tell the best stories in the world, stories not just about things he heard but things he lived too. He had been a cook, laborer, boxer, merchant marine, and like Paul Robeson (one of his heroes), a "race" man—a black man who was passionately proud of his people.

He would tell me stories about other "race" men like W. E. B. Du Bois, Jack Johnson, and the black gangster

Ellsworth Raymond "Bumpy" Johnson. He would share personal adventures about running into pirates off the coast of Cuba or being shot at by Dutch Schultz's gangsters. He told me about the Negro scientist George Washington Carver, who created over a hundred inventions from a peanut, and of Crispus Attucks, the Negro who gave his life in the American Revolution, dying before any white men. He told me wonderful stories about the South, the Caribbean, and Harlem back in their heydays; stories of Africa, the Civil War, the Spanish American War, Buffalo Soldiers, and the Black Seminole Indians of Florida.

Pa Baltimore had bad epileptic seizures that seemed to get worse, and something told me that I should spend as much time as I could with him. So each day, after I finished my homework and dinner, I would sit with him and ask him questions and listen to his stories, often even when friends called asking me to come play. When I was twelve, Pa Baltimore had a stroke and died. I was sad, but at the same time happy that I had spent time learning from him.

I didn't become truly aware of skin color until I was in the first grade, when I started walking home one of the girls in my class. She was a cute, blond-haired, blue-eyed girl named Diane. I would carry her books like a young gentleman and walk her to the corner of her block. One day I impulsively kissed Diane on the cheek. She giggled and said that now that I had kissed her, we would have to get married when we grew up. I shrugged and said, "Okay." She giggled and took her schoolbooks from me and ran into her house. The next day I waited for Diane after school. When she came out she told me that I could never walk her home again. She said that her mother told her that if we got married that we would have white babies and brown babies and that would be a sin.

After a sad, lonely walk home from school that day, I studied myself in the hallway mirror. I was brown, albeit a very light brown, probably thanks to my paternal white Spanish grandmother—"high yella," as Pa Baltimore called it. Noonie saw me on the couch sulking, and I told her what Diane's mother had said. Noonie patted my head and said that we were all God's children, that I was too young to be worried about girls, and that it was better if I stayed with "my own kind."

The first two things made sense, but her last piece of advice puzzled me. I thought I was with my own kind: human. It's not like I was trying to be with a horse or a chicken. Pa Baltimore pulled out a scrapbook and showed me a picture of an ugly, scarred, bloated black boy lying in a coffin. As I stared at the picture in horror, he explained that the boy had been murdered by redneck crackers because he had whistled at a white woman in a store. His name was Emmett Till.

That night my emotions turned from heartbreak to fear. Would the redneck crackers come and kill me because I had kissed Diane? I crept into the kitchen and got a butter knife and I finally fell asleep clutching the knife under my pillow. The next day when I saw Diane, we barely said hi.

Now all the names I had heard during my first six years of life started to register: *colored boy, dark boy, Negro, nigger.* I was a different color, and in a color-conscious society that made me different. My young mind had been jarred, and I soon picked up on other names: *coon, shine, porch monkey, black bastard.* I learned how to shout back names and fight other children who looked different: *white boy, gray boy, cracker, peckerwood, white bastard.*

One Saturday afternoon I sat in the barbershop waiting for my turn in the barber's chair. Neighborhood barbershops have been called the poor black man's country club, a place where men gather to play checkers, cards, sip beers, and swap stories. Mr. Fuller and the two other barbers were World War II veterans. They often bragged about how many trades they had learned in the army, including plumbing, auto mechanics, cooking, and barbering. But their army was a racist outfit run by "redneck cracker officers." Mr. Fuller told the story of having been part of a Negro army unit that liberated a village in France. A French woman told Mr. Fuller, in broken English, that she had heard that Negroes had tails. The whole barbershop laughed as Mr. Fuller related how he dropped his pants to show her that he had no tail—at least not in the front. The story blew my mind and made me wonder if Diane and her family thought that I was a little monkey hiding a tail.

And so it was with the five- and six-year-olds of my generation; as it was with generations before, we learned to walk, talk, read, write, and hate from our parents and elders.

The other black and brown kids around me were also doubtful, if not resentful, about their skin color. In the school yard, the biggest "sound down" (as in diss, dozens, or insult) was how black your mama was. "Your mama is so black she can go to night school and be marked absent." "Your mama is so black she sweats Bosco [chocolate syrup]." My inherited mulatto looks made me somewhat exempt from the disses, and also favored among teachers, elders, and church people. They told me I had "good hair," curly instead of nappy, and that I was cute because I had light skin. I would watch, not quite understanding, while my darker-skinned classmates got into much more trouble than I did when we were all making jokes or tossing spitballs in class.

My looks also got my ass kicked. My dark-skinned classmates would jump me in the school yard for being a "pretty boy" and a "goody-goody." When I came home with my clothes torn and a bloody nose, Noonie would ask me if the boys who jumped me were bigger than me. When I said no, she told me to go back down to the school yard and fight, because if I didn't stand up for myself people would always pick on me. And so I learned to punch, kick, wrestle, and fight. I hated the goody-goody label. Even though I was an A student, I would deliberately do things to get in trouble to prove to my roughneck friends that I was cool. The teachers didn't know what to make of me and Noonie gave me a couple of whippings trying to get my rowdy behavior in sync with my excellent grades.

The irony is that the boys who were jumping me for having curly hair couldn't wait to be old enough to burn their scalps with hair creams filled with lye so they could wear their straightened hair in a popular style known as the process. Most of the black girls and women in the neighborhood endured hot combs, chemicals, and skin-bleaching creams to become "American Beauties."

Racial slurs; gang-fighting the white boys from Eastchester Avenue; being smacked by white cops; hearing the mantra "Niggers ain't shit" from friends, parents, and elders all just seemed like a regular part of life growing up in the Bronx. The stories I heard in summer camp from black kids who lived other places, and the stories from guests at Noonie's dinner table, all led me to believe that this was normal everywhere else in America as well. It seemed like everyone from the barbers, mechanics, social workers, and teachers to even Mr. Battle, the black cop who lived in our neighborhood, felt the same way: black and white people were different, and life would always be a harder struggle because you were black.

When I was twelve years old, I was walking home from a family friend's house in Mt. Vernon, an "uburb" (urban/

suburban area) that bordered the Bronx. It was Sunday night and I decided to walk home instead of taking the bus like I was supposed to. These streets had more trees, wooded lots, and dark turns than my neighborhood. Walking them alone at night felt like a jungle expedition. I saw an owl perching on a tree in someone's front yard. He spun his head around and took off. I dived to the ground like I was being strafed by an enemy plane. The fact that the walk was scary made it even more fun. I loaded up my pockets with rocks in case I was attacked by the owl or another wild animal.

As I was crossing a small intersection two cars collided. The sound effects were worse than the actual impact. A loose bumper and a dented fender seemed to be the extent of the damage. Two white guys in their twenties got out of one car; a slightly older black guy got out of the other car. The men started looking around for a nonexistent stop sign, arguing about who had the right of way. No one seemed to notice that their cars had almost hit me. I stepped back on the curb and watched the argument heat up. One of the white guys was holding a beer can. He threw the can against the black guy's car. "Come on, we don't have to do all this," the black guy protested.

This seemed to annoy the white guys even more. They pounced on the black guy and slammed him into his own car. He lay across the hood, trying to fend off punches and kicks. "Stop," he yelled. "Help, somebody help me." Then he rolled over and looked directly at me with pleading eyes. "Help me!" he screamed.

"Don't do that," I yelled, and then I stepped off the curb and took three steps in the direction of the white guys.

One of them saw me coming and slurred, "You want some of this, nigger?" He took a drunken step toward me. I stepped back. He took another step toward me and I ran. I didn't look back for fear that the white guy would be behind me. I didn't stop running until I got home. Then I sat on the front steps of my building with tears of both fear and shame running down my face. I should have tried to fight those guys. I should have thrown a rock. I should have run for the cops. Instead I just ran. I was lame, a coward, a punk.

I listened to the AM news station on my little transistor radio that night, trying to see if there was a report on a black man who had been beaten to death by two drunk white guys. I heard nothing. The next day after school I rode by the intersection on the bus to see if there would be a chalk outline of his body on the street, like the one you see on TV cop shows. But the street was clear. I never told anyone how I ran: not Noonie, not my best friends Roy and John—no one. My shame turned into anger against white people, white men in particular. I began to truly hate my light skin and curly hair.

About the same time black men in suits and bow ties started selling papers near the train station. They called themselves Black Muslims and said that the white man was the devil.

Noonie and Pastor Lloyd, from our church, were horrified. "The devil is not white," they said. "He's invisible and he's everywhere." But I wasn't so sure. Despite the warning, I bought copies of *Muhammad Speaks* and delighted in looking at the cartoons that depicted Uncle Sam, the police, and other important white men with horns and a tail.

Sometimes the comfort of the devil image wasn't enough; I would need the soul-cleansing ritual of a good fight. The problem is that I would often pick the wrong white boy to swing on. Like Carmelo, Mr. Carlo's (the Italian numbers guy) nephew. He ran home with a bloody nose after I picked a fight with him over whether Spider-Man could beat Batman. Twenty minutes later a Thunderbird with Carmelo and his two older brothers drove up. They shoved me a couple of times and threatened to kick my ass up and down the street. I was scared but also mad, wishing I had older brothers who would come running to my rescue and beat up these guys. Finally they let me go and drove off. I always wanted to fight Carmelo, to get him back for telling, but every time I saw him near his uncle's candy store I would just nod and he would nod back.

The next summer, when I was thirteen, Noonie sent me to visit some of her relatives in Marshall, Virginia. It was my first time around horses and tractors—and outhouses. Imagine my surprise having to poop in an outhouse, that stinky wooden shack in the back of the house. There was running water inside and a water heater that could be turned on a few minutes before you took a bath, but there was no toilet. A two-lane paved road divided the black and white parts of Marshall. The whites weren't rich but had slightly bigger and nicer houses with indoor toilets. As far as I could tell, everybody in town made a living by working on one of the farms or one of the factories. Aunt Cleo and Aunt Mae, the ladies I stayed with, were retired from bookkeeping and domestic work.

The Greyhound bus dropped me near Aunt Cleo's two-story wooden house. It was morning and I had been riding all night. Aunt Cleo and her grandson, Roger, who was thirteen, met me at the bus stop. Roger showed me where to put my stuff and took me to the outhouse. When I was inside trying to do my business, he told me that snakes would sometimes crawl in there and bite people on the ass. He fell out laughing when I ran out with my dungarees half off. I was ready to fight, but he made me laugh when he drawled, "Aw, come on. Can't y'all take a joke?" We washed up and went inside for a breakfast of chicken-fried apples and grits. It was a weird breakfast, but man was it good.

I spent the next few days exploring the woods with Roger, swimming naked with four other boys in a lake, and eating peanut butter sandwiches in a secret cave. I was a regular Huck Finn. A skinny, thirteen-year-old girl named Betty, with a pretty face, would always smile at me when Roger and I walked by her front porch.

"She likes you," Roger said. "She used to like me, but I got me another girlfriend now."

"No, she don't," I said, blushing. I was still real shy when it came to girls.

"She likes you," Roger insisted. "Maybe she wants to give you some."

I looked back at the porch and she smiled again. I blushed and kept on walking.

The next day Roger and I were on Aunt Cleo's porch when Betty walked by and waved. I waved back.

"Wanna walk me to the store?" she asked.

"Me and Roger?" I yelled back.

"No, silly, just you."

"She gonna give you some," Roger teased.

"Shut up," I snapped.

"Well, go ahead. What? Are you scared?" Roger persisted.

"Hell, no," I insisted, but I was shaking like I was freezing. I hopped off of the porch and walked with Betty down the road.

On the way back from the store, Betty pulled me into the woods and kissed me. I was tight-lipped, nervous. "Relax," she said. "Open your mouth a little." She kissed me again and used her tongue to play with my tongue. Fireworks went off inside of me. If she was giving me "some," I wanted more. After a few minutes Betty led me out of the woods and back to my aunt's house. "I'll see you tomorrow," she said. "Don't tell nobody." I could hardly sleep that night, thinking about Betty and the woods.

The next day the black kids and the white kids played softball in the field across the road from my aunt's house. It was on the white side of the road. A twelve-year-old white kid named Dale bossed everybody around, especially the black kids. Dale called kids names like "stupid" and "blind" when they would miss a hit or drop a ball, and his arrogance and southern drawl really annoyed me. When it was my turn at bat, I swung at the ball and missed. Strike one. Another ball was pitched to me. Strike two. Dale was standing by first base. "Hit the ball, stupid," he said. "Don't just stand there like a beanpole." That's all it took for me to run over and sock him in the nose. I balled my fist, ready for a good fight, but Dale got up, cupped his hand over his bloody nose, and ran across the field to his house.

My cousin Roger came over to me. "Whatcha do that for?" he asked.

"Cuz he came out his mouth wrong," I replied with my tough New York attitude.

Nobody wanted to play after that. So Roger and I walked across the road to my auntie's house. I hung around the porch, hoping to see Betty, until my aunt called us in for lunch. As we were eating sandwiches, a car and a pickup truck pulled up in front of the house and six tough-looking white men got out. My aunt went out to meet them. The white men seemed angry; my aunt seemed nervous. Roger and I peeked through the front door. Aunt Cleo saw me and called for me to come out of the house. As I walked to Aunt Cleo I saw Dale standing with the white men. "You hit this boy while y'all was playing ball?" Aunt Cleo said angrily. "Apologize right now!"

"But he called me names," I protested.

Aunt Cleo grabbed my arm and shook me. "Apologize or I'll beat the tan off you."

"I'm sorry," I said to Dale. "I didn't mean it." Dale nodded. The other white men looked stern.

"Go back in the house," Aunt Cleo ordered.

I went inside and picked at the remainder of my lunch. Through the kitchen window I saw the white men's car and pickup truck pull away. Aunt Cleo was in the kitchen a moment later. "I'm putting you on the bus today. You're about to get yourself killed down here. Them were the Ku Klux Klan," she said, wringing her hands. "Dale is the Grand Dragon's son."

Within two hours my suitcase was packed and I was standing by the roadside Greyhound bus stop near my auntie's house. The bus came. My aunt and my cousins hugged me and I got on. As the bus pulled off I saw Betty walking down the road. I knocked on the window. She smiled and waved. Damn, I thought as the bus headed up the highway, the South is crazy.

3

Finding the Panther Lair

I walked into a Panther office in Brooklyn in September 1968. Dr. King had been assassinated in April of that year. Riots and anger flared in ghettos around the country. The feeling on the street was that the shit was about to hit the fan. "Black power" was the phrase of the day, and hating "whitey" was the hip thing to do. From street corner speeches to campus rallies, whitey had gone from being "the Man" to being "the Beast." Young black students were trading in their feel-good

Motown Records for the recorded speeches of Malcolm X and the angry jazz recordings of Ornette Coleman.

I went down to 125th Street in Harlem the night that Dr. King was assassinated. Protesters and rioters swarmed the streets, clashing with cops, overturning cars, setting trash can fires, and hurling bricks at white-owned businesses. One of the storefront windows was shattered by an airborne trash can. Looters ran into the store and started taking clothes, appliances, and whatever else they could carry.

Not everyone looted—in fact, most of the crowd continued to chant "The king is dead" and "Black power"—but it was enough for the cops to start swinging clubs, shooting their pistols, and making arrests. A cop grabbed me and threw me against the wall. Before he could handcuff me and put me in the paddy wagon, a group of rioters across the street turned a police car over. The cop told me to stay put and ran toward the rioters.

I was scared, but I wasn't stupid. I took off running in the opposite direction. I blended in with a group of rioters and tried to figure out which way to go. A group of cops headed toward us. Some of the rioters ran into a clothing store that was being looted. I followed. The cops entered the store swinging clubs and making arrests. My heart pounded as I ran into the back of the store and found a back door leading to an alley. I gasped for air as I ran down the alley and was stopped by a wooden fence. The cops came into the alley. "Halt," they yelled. "Put your hands up." In my mind I froze, put my hands in the air, and turned around to face the cops with tears in my eyes. But my body kept hauling ass. I grabbed the fence and scurried over the top like a scared alley cat. Two shots rang out. One splintered the wood on the fence near my butt. This gave me the fear/adrenaline push I needed to flip over the fence, pick myself up off the ground, and scramble out of the alley.

When I turned out on the street, I kept running, right past two other cops who tried to grab me, but I jerked away. Turning the corner, I almost collided with a group of twenty or so black men in leather coats and army fatigue jackets, wearing Afros and berets, standing on the corner in a military-like formation. "Stop running, young brother," one of the men with a beard and tinted glasses said. "Don't give these pigs an excuse to gun you down." I doubled over, heaving, trying to catch my breath. I didn't know this man, but his voice sounded like a life raft of confidence in a sea of chaos.

Moments later two cops ran around the corner. They stopped in their tracks when they saw the militant men. The men closed ranks around me. "What are you doing here?" one of the cops demanded. "Move aside."

The black man with the tinted glasses didn't flinch. "We're exercising our constitutional right to free assembly. Making sure no innocent people get killed out here tonight."

"We're chasing looters," the cop retorted.

"No looters here. As you can see, we're a disciplined community patrol."

"You have guns?" the cop asked, a tinge of fear in his voice.

"That's what you said," the man with tinted glasses replied. "I said we're exercising our constitutional rights." The cops took in the size and discipline of the group for a moment and walked away.

By this time I'd caught my breath, but I was speechless from what I had just seen: black men standing down white cops. "Go straight home, young brother," the man with the tinted glasses said. "The pigs are looking for any excuse to murder black folks tonight." With that, the black men walked on. I scooted down to the subway and rode home. When I entered the apartment, Noonie was sitting on the couch watching images of Dr. King on TV. Tears fell from her eyes. She didn't even ask me where I had been, which was unusual since I was about two hours late getting home. I sat next to her and put my arm around her, and we watched the TV reports of the assassination and the riots.

By July 1968 the country was still smoldering with the hot embers of social change, but in the hills of Camp Minisink, located in upstate New York, kids and teens from Harlem were just happy to enjoy campfires and swimming in a lake, miles away from the melting asphalt of their home. Camp Minisink was the oldest African American camp in New York State. I had a job there as a junior counselor. I was also part of one of Minisink's youth organizations known as the Order of the Feather.

Young men who wanted to join the Order of the Feather had to pledge six months before becoming "Feathermen," earning the right to wear the coveted maroon and white varsity-style sweater of the organization. The fraternity was modeled after the Boy Scouts Order of the Arrow and after black college fraternities. Although we were young, becoming part of the organization was a tough, disciplined, and challenging rite-of-passage process.

We "pledgees" had to wear white shirts and maroon bow ties as uniforms, march in a precision line, address all Feathermen as "sir" or "big brother," and do push-ups and other forms of "creative punishment" when we failed at a task or bungled an assignment. We had to read black history books (or "Negro" history as many in the community still called it), turn in written assignments, bring in our report cards, and attend career and education workshops. Pledgees were not allowed to go to parties, have girlfriends, smoke, or drink.

I took the pledgee oath in Minisink's Harlem Community Center along with 150 other young men. By the time we got to camp for the last few weeks of the training process, there were only thirty-five of us. A lot of guys quit or had been dismissed from the line by the older Feathermen for being slack. The idea was that if you could cross "the burning sands" of the pledge process and become a Featherman, then you could meet any challenge that life held for you as a young Negro man, and you could succeed. Most Feathermen went on to college and became successful in professions ranging from teaching and medicine to law enforcement.

But a lot of us pledged because the Feathermen were so damn cool. All the cute girls in camp wanted to date Feathermen. Plus the Feathermen could order the pledgees to grab their food trays, do their cabin chores, and sing off-key circus songs to make their girlfriends laugh. How cool was that?

For me and a lot of other teenage boys, the Feather represented a path to manhood. In fact, the Order of the Feather founders created the program in 1946 as a way to challenge the gang epidemic in Harlem. Their alternative was simply this: you could go through a one-night gang initiation, receive your gang jacket, and go through life ducking and dodging the cops and rival gang members, or you could go through a rigorous but positive six-month initiation and proudly wear your Featherman sweater at school, church, or any place in the community. While the Feather program didn't eradicate the gangs, a number of boys left or avoided gangs to become Feathermen.

Two older Feathermen who lived in my neighborhood, James, nineteen, and Eric, eighteen, gave me hell while I was pledging. I had to go to their house to do their chores and pick up their food trays in the high school lunchroom. They also made me run up to girls around school, then bend on one knee and recite corny sonnets. The girls giggled as I earnestly recited the lines the big brothers had instructed me to deliver in my best Shakespearean style, all of it romantic and silly and very, very innocent.

When the school bus full of pledgees and Feathermen arrived in the rolling hills of Camp Minisink, things got worse. As a junior counselor I worked all day but would often be pulled from an exhausted sleep at night for push-ups and work details given by James, Eric, and other Feathermen. In a final rite-of-passage ceremony called Tap Out, we pledgees stood bare-chested around a large bonfire and received an initiation tap in the chest by Feathermen dressed in Native American and African costumes. The next night we received our Feather sweaters at a banquet in the camp dining hall. James and Eric were among the first two Feathermen to embrace me and welcome me into the organization.

"You guys gave me hell," I said, confused by the sudden warmth they showed me.

"That's because we like you," James replied. "If you like a dude, you always pledge him harder. Plus you made us laugh."

From that night on I hung out with James and Eric. When they weren't on duty as counselors, they swapped their camp T-shirts for African dashikis and hung out in their cabin featuring Black Power posters, incense, a stereo that played Miles Davis and Malcolm X records, and a red lightbulb that gave their cabin the feel of being a black militant speakeasy in the woods.

Because of James and Eric, I got into the fashion side of black militancy first. I grew a big Afro and dressed in bell-bottoms and dashikis. My skinny fifteen-year-old butt looked like a five-foot-eleven black Q-tip. At the end of the summer, H. Rap Brown came to speak at a youth conference at Camp Minisink. The younger campers had all gone home and the cabins were now filled with high school and college students who were up for the weekend attending youth leadership workshops. H. Rap Brown was the conference keynote speaker. He was often in the news as a militant leader who dismissed integration and stood for black nationalism.

I was blown away by his whole style: the 'fro; the shades; the finger that jabbed the air like a Zulu spear when he spoke, slicing up white America. Wow, man, Rap could rap. "You been brainwashed. You wear white to weddings, black to funerals. Angel food cake is white cake. Devil's food cake is black. White magic is good. Black magic is evil. In cowboy movies the good guys wear the white hats and the bad guys wear black. Even Santa Claus. I mean, tell me how in the hell a fat, camel-breath redneck honkie can slide down a black chimney and still come out white? I'm telling you, you been brainwashed." The crowd of three hundred high school and college students attending the conference went wild; we cheered Rap Brown like a rock star.

Right then and there I decided to embrace militancy. My friend Phil teased me on the way back to our cabin that night. "You can't announce you're going to be a black militant like it's a career choice. It's a belief, not a job." But my mind was made up. Rap Brown lived in the South, but I would find other black militants to hook up with when I got back to New York City.

I came from camp with an Afro, wearing a dashiki, and inserting "black power" in every sentence I could, even if I was ordering ice cream. ("Give me some of those black-power sprinkles on that cone, my brother.") I started looking for a black militant organization to join, going about it the way high school seniors scope out colleges. Since I had no real political consciousness, I entertained and rejected organizations for the most subjective reasons. The Black Muslims? Nah, I don't really like bow ties and I do like a piece of bacon every now and then. SNCC (Student National Coordinating Committee)? No, that sounds too close to "snake," and my friends who love to play the dozens would have a ball with that.

One night, while sitting on the couch watching Noonie's old black-and-white TV, I saw a news report on the Black Panther Party. Footage was shown of the Panthers, with guns, storming a session of the California State Legislature. California was about to change its laws by making it illegal to carry firearms, and the Panthers burst into the room calling the legislature racist for wanting to take away black people's constitutional right to arm themselves for the purpose of self-defense. The old white politicians I saw on the TV screen looked scared to death. The cops who moved in on the Panthers looked confused and subdued as the Panthers shouted, "Go ahead and arrest me, pig, or get the hell out of my face." Since the guns were legal, the only thing the police could do was eject the Panthers from the legislative chambers.

Then a reporter came on the TV talking about the Black Panther Party as an ultramilitant, dangerous organization. He cited an incident earlier that day in which the police had found a trunk full of guns and communist literature in a Black Panther's car. My jaw dropped as I watched the news report. Look at those dudes, I thought. They're crazy. They got black leather coats and berets, carrying guns, scaring white people, reading communist books. They're *crazy*. I immediately wanted to join. I hopped around the living room, freaking out with excitement. I had found my organization, my cause. Now all I had to do was find out where the Black Panthers were in New York.

Like a plantation slave seeking passage to freedom on the Underground Railroad, I put out the word that I was looking to hook up with the Panthers. Not that my network was particularly sophisticated, but I did ask anybody and everybody who I thought might have a lead: the bad dudes who hung out on the corner and on the basketball courts; Mr. Sunny, the neighborhood numbers runner; Mr. Pete, the neighborhood wino; and Blue, the neighborhood junkie. Word about the Panthers came back in hushed tones. They were extreme militants who existed in secret. You didn't choose the Panthers. They chose you. So I walked around acting extra cool and extra militant, hoping that some Panther secret agent would tap me on the shoulder and guide me to their headquarters.

One Saturday James and Eric eased up next to me in the park while I was waiting my turn to play basketball.

"Dude's sayin' you runnin' around lookin' for the Panthers," Eric said.

"Yeah, man," I replied.

"Well, first of all be cool with that shit. You can't let everybody know your business." Eric looked around to see if anybody was watching or listening. Then he leaned closer. "The Panthers have an office in Brooklyn. We're rollin' out there tomorrow. Are you down?"

"I'm down," I replied too loudly. Eric gave me a stern look.

"I keep telling you to be cool with this shit. Meet us here at one o'clock tomorrow."

I nodded. James pointed at my blue jeans and my Converse sneakers. "You gotta dress in all black and wear a leather coat. That's how the Black Panthers dress." He turned and walked away. Eric followed.

That night I could barely sleep imagining what it would be like to walk into the Panther headquarters. Would I have to fight a six-foot-three Black Panther commando to prove myself? Would I be blindfolded and taken to some secret chamber to be initiated? Maybe I'd get put on a small airplane and be parachuted into a hidden training camp somewhere in Africa.

"Boy, you better get up. Do you know what time it is?"

I opened my eyes and saw Noonie standing over me. Somewhere between my visions of the Panther initiation chamber and the parachute jump into Africa I had conked out and overslept. I glanced at my alarm clock. It was already seven fifteen. "Sorry, ma'am," I said while running to the bathroom.

Noonie was sitting at the kitchen table reading her Bible in the morning sunlight. This was her daily ritual: up at 6 a.m., morning prayers, freshen up, make me a simple breakfast, and read the Bible at the table while I ate. Noonie was no joke when it came to school, church, and discipline. She was born Jessie Mae Allen in 1898 in a poor and segregated section of North Carolina called Blue Haven, and she grew up on a farm that had been a plantation that her parents worked on as slaves. After Emancipation her parents and her nine brothers and sisters worked as sharecroppers.

Noonie told me stories of walking to school barefoot until she was eight years old and working in the tobacco fields until the sun went down. She told me how colored folks could not look white people in the eye and how they had to get off the sidewalk to let them pass. Noonie told me how white men in sheets lynched people they considered to be "uppity niggers."

One such uppity nigger was Noonie's favorite uncle, who got beaten, lynched, and burned for striking a white man who had spit tobacco in his face.

When Noonie was fourteen she had saved enough money to buy a train ticket to Harlem. She married Pa Baltimore four years later. They were together for sixty years until Pa passed away. For the last three years it had been Noonie and me in our modest Bronx apartment. When I was little she told me I could call her Nana for Grandma or Noonie, the name she had called her grandmother. I chose Noonie.

Noonie took me to Sunday school and church every Sunday morning. She was very religious, and church was the center of her life. She believed that shined shoes, clean fingernails, and the niceties "please" and "thank you" would take a person far in life. Although she only had a sixth-grade education, she could read well and spoke in accent-free English, developed from her years of housekeeping in white households.

Despite her experience when she was young, Noonie was not afraid of white people. When I was five years old I was coming home with Noonie from a church event when suddenly I had to pee so badly that I started crying. Noonie avoided an accident by unzipping my pants and letting me do my business between two parked cars. A burly white cop came along and threatened to write a summons. Her five-foot-two frame seemed to elongate as she got in the cop's face and tongue-lashed him about the mayor and the city closing public bathrooms and forcing poor kids to pee on the street. After a few minutes the cop tipped his hat, said, "Sorry, ma'am," and got out of there, moving as fast as he could. On the other hand, Noonie would literally cross the street or get off the bus to break up a fight or to scold black kids for using disrespectful language.

She was a follower of Dr. Martin Luther King Jr. and believed that love and peaceful protest were the tools for equality.

When Stokely Carmichael and H. Rap Brown would appear on the TV news screaming about black power, Noonie would shake her head and talk about those ruffians in the raggedy clothes who needed haircuts. Afros, bell-bottoms, rock music, and hippies protesting the war were not Noonie's thing. "The world is going crazy," she would tell me, "so make sure you stay on the straight and narrow and get your education." Although the Black Panther Party never came up in our conversations, I knew that me being part of an organization whose members carried guns and called the cops "pigs" would have her speaking in tongues and turning colors.

On the morning of my planned visit to the Black Panthers, I slipped past Noonie to the closet and grabbed the black leather jacket she had given me for Christmas. Noonie brought me to a halt without looking up from her Bible.

"Where you going?" she asked.

"To school," I answered, hoping not to seem like an escaping convict caught in the guard-tower searchlight.

"Just like that? Without saying good-bye?" I walked over to Noonie and kissed her on the cheek, hoping that now I could make my move out the door.

Noonie gestured toward the scrambled eggs, juice, and corn flakes on the table. "Now sit down and eat your breakfast."

"But I'm late," I said.

"That's right. You were late getting up. But I was not late when it came to making your breakfast and this food is not going to waste. There are hungry children in Africa." Noonie turned the page on her Bible.

"Then let the children in Africa eat it," I mumbled.

Noonie's eyes shot up from the Bible. "What did you say?"

"Nothing," I said meekly. I sat down and started to inhale the food.

"Slow down."

Then Noonie took in my outfit. "Why do you have on your good leather coat? And why are you dressed in all black? You going to a funeral?"

I groped for an answer. "It's Assembly Day."

Noonie wasn't buying it. "I thought you wore a white shirt to assembly."

I fished around in my oatmeal so she couldn't see my eyes searching for a comeback. "I do, except today is Armistice Day and Mr. Seawell wants the color guard to dress in black out of respect for all those who gave their lives. Bye, Noonie."

I jumped up and kissed her on the cheek, then headed out

the door, praying she wouldn't see through my lame story. As I pulled the apartment door shut behind me, I heard Noonie's footsteps on the other side of the door. Would she yank it open and call me back? I wondered. I paused, then heard her lock the door. I'd made it!

I got through the morning classes without paying attention. Then, when the bell rang for the last one, I headed into the hallway with the other students, looked for a side exit, and slipped out the door. I was cutting lunch and the rest of my classes for the day. I didn't care if I was being marked absent. In fact, I didn't even write down any of the homework assignments that day. I was going to join the Panthers, and if the teachers messed with me I would bring a battalion of the brothers into the school. We would storm the place with guns the same way I'd seen the Panthers storm the California State Legislature a few weeks earlier.

James and Eric flanked me as we sat on the subway train headed to Brooklyn. It was an hour's ride from our stop in the Bronx, plenty of time for doubt and apprehension to build.

"You sure you ready for this?" James grilled. "Panthers don't play. In fact, the Panthers be taking heads if you're not serious."

"I'm ready," I replied, trying to be as cool as possible.

"How are you ready? You still use your slave name, 'Eddie.' I know that rhymes with 'ready,' but you ain't really ready until you have an African name. My name is Rhaheem now."

Eric nodded his head in agreement. "And my name is Sabu. What's your black name?" he asked.

"I don't have one," I said, feeling like a total sap. "Can you give me one?"

"Let me see," James said, closing his eyes in deep meditation. "Yeah. We're going to call you Unbutu."

"Unbutu," I stammered.

"Usa," James said.

"Usa," I replied, confused now.

"Jamal," James said and nodded firmly.

"Ja Mal," I repeated phonetically.

"Yep, Unbutu Usa Jamal, that's your name."

"What does it mean?" I asked.

"What it means is he who comes together in the spirit of blackness."

I would find out later that James—excuse me, Rhaheem—was totally pulling syllables and meanings out of the air, but at that moment, sitting in a subway car headed for Brooklyn, I had been reborn and renamed. I smiled to myself as we rode. I had a black name and a black outfit. I was almost a Panther—and we hadn't even gotten to headquarters yet.

Then Rhaheem leaned over to me and said in a low voice, "You know, the Panthers are like the Mafia. Once you join, there's no getting out."

"I don't care," I responded nonchalantly, though inside I was feeling unsure.

Sabu leaned in. "Man, you know you gotta kill a white dude in order to be a Panther."

"I don't care," I said with a shrug. Now I was really feeling nervous. Kill somebody? Just to join? But I was with two of the coolest guys from the neighborhood, and I couldn't let them think I was a punk.

"Naw, get it straight," James said indignantly. "You don't have to kill a white dude." With those words I began to breathe again and I felt myself relax. "You have to kill a white cop," he said, "and you have to bring in his badge and his gun."

All the air sucked out my lungs, and my stomach felt like an erupting volcano. But I couldn't be a punk. "I don't care," I squeaked, and sat back between James and Eric, suddenly feeling like a condemned man.

We got off the subway at Nostrand Avenue and walked toward the Panther office. The closer we got, the more my spine began to rattle. Suppose the Panthers killed us just for daring to show up on their doorstep. I was hoping that one of my friends would chump out first. I could tell that we were all nervous, but none of us wanted to be the one who got teased for bitchin' up. As we approached the office, we saw the Panther logo and the sign BLACK PANTHER PARTY. We walked up to the front door and were greeted warmly by a stunningly beautiful woman in a long African dress. That was enough to get the three of us inside.

We passed posters of Huey P. Newton and Bobby Seale, both men holding guns. A burly man in a beret and a leather jacket welcomed us with a "Power to the people" greeting. We imitated his black-power salute and answered, "Power."

He pointed out three empty chairs at the back of the room. The office was packed with about fifty men and women, some wearing Panther uniforms, some wearing African garb. Everyone was "militant cool." My heart began to race with excitement. I had made it to the inner sanctum.

The meeting was being run by a handsome twenty-five-year-old man in shades and a leather jacket, seated behind a large wooden desk. People addressed him as Lieutenant Edmay or brother lieutenant. He was reading from the back page of the Black Panther Party newspaper, which listed the Ten-Point Program. After each point he would take comments from Panthers in the room. As I looked about, everyone in the room seemed older, but then I had just turned fifteen, so everyone *was* older. The Panthers in this meeting ranged in age from eighteen to twenty-five. They were students, ex-convicts, Vietnam veterans, welfare mothers, street people, the disenfranchised, the least opposing the most, the folks that Malcolm X called "the grassroots." "Point number one," Lieutenant Edmay recited, "we want freedom. We want the power to determine the destiny of our community." There was some discussion on the point, and Edmay moved on. "Number two," he continued, "we want full employment for our people. Number three, we want an end to the robbery by the capitalists of our black community."

The Panthers in the room made comments about human rights, equal justice, better housing, community action

programs, and other ways to improve things in the community. There was no conversation about murdering white people, blood oaths, and general acts of mayhem. But I couldn't
really hear what was being said because I had my own internal
adolescent conversation raging in my head, a kind of mantra,
with me reciting, "I'm a man. I ain't no punk." By the time
Edmay got through a few more points, I had hyped myself up
to make my bid to be a Panther.

"Number seven, we want an end to police brutality and the
murder of our people."

That was my cue. I jumped to my feet. "Choose me,
brother," I shouted. "Arm me and send me on a mission. I'll
kill whitey right now." Edmay looked at me long and hard and
gestured for me to come to the front. I looked at my friends
with an expression that said, "I told you I was ready." They
looked amazed. I walked to the front of the office, under the
silent and intense scrutiny of dozens of Panthers.

Lieutenant Edmay inspected me for a moment. Then
he pulled open the bottom drawer of the bottom desk and
reached deep inside. My heart began pounding again. Damn,
I thought, look how far he's reaching in that drawer. He must
be pulling out a big ass gun. Instead Edmay handed me a
small stack of books. *The Autobiography of Malcolm X, Soul
on Ice* by Eldridge Cleaver, *The Wretched of the Earth* by
Frantz Fanon, and the "Little Red Book" by Mao Tse-tung.

I gazed at the books and looked stupidly around the room.
Books? I played hooky to come here. If I wanted books I would

have stayed in school today. This must be a test, I decided. So I cocked my head to the side and slurred my voice like a black militant James Cagney. "Excuse me, brother, I thought you said you were going to arm me."

"Excuse me, young brother, I just did." There were shouts of "Power to the people!" and "Right on!" which I later found out was a revolutionary version of "amen."

I felt embarrassed as I hung my head and walked toward my seat. Then Lieutenant Edmay called out to me: "Young brother." I froze and turned around. "Let me ask you a question." He launched into an articulation and cadence unique and famous to the Black Panther Party. "What if all of the racist-pig police running amok in the community, wantonly brutalizing and shooting down people, were black and the people being murdered were white? What if all of these greedy-hog avaricious businessmen who are ripping off the community and selling people this rotting food and these jive-time inferior products were black and the people being ripped off were white? What if all of these fascist-swine and imperialist-demagogue politicians were black and the people who were colonized, oppressed, and stomped down were white? Would that make things correct?"

I thought hard for a moment. Something told me the answer from my heart instead of from my militant Afro or my adolescent ego. "No, brother, I guess it would still be wrong."

"That's right," said Edmay, smiling for the first time. "This is a class struggle, not just a race struggle. We're not fighting a skin color; we're fighting a corrupt capitalist system that exploits all poor people. Study those books so you can learn what the revolution is really about."

I was humbled as I returned to my seat. I spent the rest of the meeting really paying attention to what was being said about the Ten-Point Program and the Panthers' demands for an end to police brutality and a decent standard of living for poor and struggling folks.

As we were leaving the Panther office, I was stopped by a beautiful woman with dark brown skin and short hair. I had learned during the meeting that her name was Afeni Shakur and that she was a Panther leader. She had been outspoken during the PE (political education) class, saying that part-time revolutionaries and bourgeois Negroes who just wanted to look cool in a Panther uniform should get their asses out the office right now. "The struggle," she said, "is about love, sacrifice, and being willing to die for the people."

After the meeting I was at the front desk looking at copies of the Black Panther Party newspaper. Afeni walked over and stood in front of me. "How old are you?" she asked.

"Sixteen," I answered, jacking my age up a year.

"You look like you're thirteen, maybe fourteen. Go home."

"I'm sixteen and a half," I snapped back, trying to hide my desperation, thinking maybe another half year on the lie would make a difference.

"I said go home," Afeni replied with unblinking firmness. I swallowed, and my next words came from nowhere as though a ventriloquist were using me as his skinny fifteen-year-old dummy. "I'm not going home," I said firmly. "I want to be a Panther."

Afeni looked me up and down, from head to toe. "Then make sure I see you every time you come in the office. I got my eye on you." With that she was off, talking shop with a group of senior Panthers in another part of the office.

James, Eric, and I purchased some Panther papers and stepped out of the office. We were stopped by a man standing six-foot-one, in fighting shape and wearing dark shades even though it was nighttime. "Where you brothers from?" he asked.

"Africa," James replied.

"And is the subway taking your African ass home to Nigeria tonight? Or you crashing somewhere here in the city?" Yedwa asked with a sly smile.

"I live in the Bronx." James answered. "For now," he added, trying to salvage his ego.

Yedwa looked at Eric and me. "You all from the Bronx too?" he inquired.

"Yes, brother," we replied.

"Right on. That means I'm your section leader. My name is Yedwa. The next PE class is on Saturday. Make sure you know the Ten-Point Program. Power to the people." The subway ride home was quiet. We read Panther papers and tried to digest the events of the last three hours.

"All power to the people," a fiery Panther speaker named

Dhoruba had said in the PE class. "That means black power to black people, white power to white people, brown power to brown people, red power to red people, yellow power to yellow people, and Panther power to the vanguard."

"Right on," the room replied with pumped fists. "Power to the people and death to the fascist pigs."

"Pigs" was the name the Panthers had for the cops, the businessmen, the politicians, and anyone who was part of the ruling power structure. The power structure, as it was explained in the PE class, was a capitalist system that profited the rich and oppressed the poor, the Proletarians. I went to the Panther office saying I hated "whitey," and I came out talking about Marx, Lenin, Mao, and Che Guevara. This was new, exciting, and really confusing. I had grown up learning to fear, distrust, and yet admire white people. At the same time, I had learned to be self-conscious and sometimes hateful toward my blackness. Now I had to rethink everything.

4

A Panther Is a Two-Legged Cat

I could read well and was a good student. So memorizing the Panther Ten-Point Program by the next meeting was no problem. James, Eric, and I reported to the new Harlem office, which was on Seventh Avenue and 122nd Street. Captain Lumumba Shakur ran the meeting, and when he called on me I recited the Ten-Point Program flawlessly. "Point number ten. We want land, bread, housing, education, justice, and peace. And as our major political objective a United Nations supervised plebiscite that will determine the will of Black people as to their National destiny."

"Right on," the other Panthers in the meeting said. "Good job, brother."

I sat down, feeling proud. I was now officially a Panther in training. After the meeting I spotted a cute Panther sister who appeared to be around eighteen. She smiled. I puffed my chest out and walked over. "What's happening, baby?" I said coolly.

Her smile turned into a military stare. "The revolution is happening, brother, and I'm nobody's baby." The young Panther sister walked off. I didn't notice Yedwa standing two feet away, but he saw the whole thing.

"You can't run a jive-time game on a Panther woman," he scolded. "You got to greet her with respect. You say, 'Power to the people, my sister.' She says, 'Power to the people, my brother. How are you doing?' Then you say, 'Aw, I'm really exhausted, my sister. I've been working hard for the people. Selling newspapers, organizing, doing community patrols, political education class. Just trying to make the revolution happen.'" I nodded dumbly. "Matter of fact," Yedwa said, "you and your boys from the Bronx meet me in Central Park Saturday morning at eight a.m. for some training." Yedwa shook his head and walked away. Once again I left the Panther office feeling unsure of myself.

Over the next few weeks Yedwa and a couple of other senior

Panthers led us through military-style calisthenics, hand-to-hand combat techniques, and security detail training. We also learned how to sell Panther newspapers and organizing techniques. I went along with Afeni as she organized tenants to have rent strikes. I also watched her organize parents and progressive teachers in Harlem schools. I used these techniques in my school to form a black students organization and to get black and white students to march out of school in protest of the Vietnam War.

One day after political education class, Yedwa pulled me to the side. "You're doing good, Brother Jamal. Now that you're getting your PE down, it's time for you to learn about TE." TE stood for technical equipment, which stood for guns. Yedwa made me memorize his address and told me to be at his house at 6 p.m. When I knocked on his door that evening Yedwa answered holding a .44 automatic pistol. Sadik and Katara were already in the living room. "Power to the people," I said. "Power, brother," they replied.

Yedwa went to his closet and pulled out a green army duffel bag. He reached inside and pulled out an M16 rifle. "First thing you know about a gun," he said, "is to never point it at anyone unless you intend to kill them." He showed me how to unload the gun, clear the chamber, and put the safety on. Then he handed me the rifle and my training began. After an hour or so of taking apart different weapons, Yedwa handed me the M16 and said, "Good. Now do it blindfolded."

The next three months became more and more about the Panthers and less and less about school, church, and my other activities. I stopped doing karate and the after-school teen program at Minisink Townhouse (a community center in Harlem). I stopped singing in the choir and would slip out of church services early. "Religion is the opium of the masses," Mao Tse-tung said in the "Little Red Book," and so rather than worship with Noonie, I'd spend my Sundays on 125th Street enlightening the masses by selling copies of the Black Panther newspaper.

School became a battleground. I had skipped the eighth grade as part of a program they had in New York City schools known as Special Progress. I was now in the eleventh grade at age 15. My plan had been to graduate high school at sixteen, get a scholarship and finish college in three years, and go to law school and be an attorney by twenty-one. Then I would make a lot of money and buy Noonie a big house next to mine in the suburbs. My second-grade teacher, a firm but loving woman named Mrs. Johnson, had once told Noonie that I was the best student in her class and that I would grow up to be president one day. Noonie smiled with pride and gave me a big hug.

So I thought that after being an attorney for a few years I would go into politics and be a congressman or a senator. Even before joining the Panthers I had been disabused of the notion that I or any other black kid could grow up to be president, but maybe a congressman or a senator was possible.

But by November of 1968 I was a full-fledged Panther de-termined to point out all the contradictions in the capitalis-tic bourgeois educational system. Forget going to college. I wanted to lead the students and instill a revolutionary cur-riculum in the high schools in New York. I was convinced that by the time I was supposed to go to college the people's revolution would be in full swing, and I would be in heavy combat against the army and the national guard as we battled for the liberation of Harlem, the South Bronx, and other black colonies across the country.

At the same time, the white students I had been organizing in my high school would be waging war in their own commu-nities, which we (the Panthers) called "the mother country." If there were any colleges functioning, they would be People's Universities that would teach classes in Socialist economics, medicine, agriculture, and other subjects relevant to building a new revolutionary society. So imagine me in a classroom with a teacher trying to present a lesson about slavery and Reconstruction. I'd spend the whole period talking about slavery's connection to capitalism and the heroic actions of the rebel slave Nat Turner and the white abolitionist John Brown. When I wasn't challenging my history teacher about American imperialism or my English teacher about the racist and bourgeois nature of the writings of Mark Twain, I would be organizing school rallies and walkouts demanding a black studies program or an end to the war in Vietnam.

My grades started slipping and letters were sent home to Noonie about my "behavior problems." I would intercept these letters and toss them into the trash can. I guess the school also tried to call Noonie at home, but she still did domestic work a few hours during the day and didn't get home till after five o'clock.

I'd go to the Panther office every day after school and be there all day Saturday and most of Sunday. The Panther office was one part political field office and three parts counseling center. People from the community would come to the Panther office for all kinds of problems. "Cops are kicking a guy's ass down the block," a man would scream, running into the office. In ten seconds we would be on the move, running down the street and forming a protective wall between the cops and the black man they were roughing up. More cops would come, more community people would come. Sometimes the cops would back off; sometime they would make an arrest and we would follow them to the precinct to make sure that there was no more police brutality and that the black person who was arrested had a lawyer.

One day a mother came in carrying her ten-year-old daughter, who was moaning and shaking. "She has sickle-cell anemia," her mother said. "I went to the hospital and they sent me home. They told me that it was psychosomatic. That I should just give my daughter some aspirin and put her in bed."

Within minutes we were back in the hospital emergency

room with the mother and her daughter—thirty Panthers in uniform, looking poised and dangerous. The white doctors and nurses looked at us and their jaws dropped. "You better treat this young sister right now," Captain Lumumba Shakur demanded, "or there's going to be a psychosomatic riot right here in the emergency room." The ER doctors located a hematologist and gave the little girl morphine for her pain and proper treatment for her sickle-cell. I stood at attention in line with the other Panthers, but inside I was bursting with excitement and pride. I had never seen or been a part of anything like this. Young black people, liberation soldiers, taking on doctors and the hospital system—and winning. I felt like I was part of a team of superheroes, like I might even been able to step outside and fly.

One day I was with Afeni and other Panthers in a broken-down building whose tenants we were helping to organize. I saw a little boy with a bandage covering an ugly rat bite. We noticed a baby sleeping in a crib with panties tied around his head. "Why do you have panties around the baby's head?" Afeni asked the young mother.

"So the roaches won't crawl into her nose or her ears while she sleeps," the young mother replied tearfully. "I scrub my house every day. I use the insect spray every night, and they still come back."

By the end of the week we helped the tenants seize control of the building and had community lawyers teach them how to set up an escrow account so they could use their rent money to bring in an exterminator and make repairs to the building.

It felt like there was never a dull moment with the Black Panther Party. I was always in the midst of excitement, potential danger, and the coolest black men and women on the planet. What fifteen-year-old wouldn't want to feel as fully engaged and as turned on about life, black culture, and the "people's revolution" as I was?

The New York chapter was divided into sections according to where you lived. The Bronx section did not have an office. We went to our main meetings at the Harlem office but had section meetings at Yedwa's house. There were about fifteen of us in a section. I would find reasons to hang around and be one of the last ones to leave the meeting. I was fascinated by Yedwa's swagger and style. He spent time in Vietnam before joining the movement. He worked along with Lumumba Shakur as an organizer for a group called the Elsmere Tenants Council. They would help tenants get repairs, heat, fight evictions, and so forth.

Yedwa was always shoving cops, arguing with officials, and talking about battling the pigs. Most of the young Panthers wanted to be like him. I felt really cool and important when Yedwa would let me hang around with him selling Panther papers; standing security at a rally; or cooling out in his apartment listening to jazz, eating fried chicken and apple pie, and talking about life from a "revolutionary black man's point of view."

His pad had a couch with no legs and a couple of pillows that Yedwa called the "low-to-the-ground feel." He would push back his couch to teach me fighting moves or take me to the park and show me hand-to-hand combat techniques. He took me to the woods and taught me how to shoot a pistol and a rifle so I could be "ready when the time comes." Most important, for a fifteen-year-old man-child with raging hormones, he instructed me on the right way to rap to a Panther woman, something he had touched on earlier when he overheard me trying to talk to a pretty young sister. Yedwa completed the lesson with a smile and a wink. "If you say all the right things, then a sister might tell you, 'Well, come by my house and rest while I make a little dinner, brother.' See Panther women like brothers who work hard for the struggle. That's how you get their attention."

I first got Yedwa's attention when the Panthers got into a scuffle with cops at a courthouse in Brooklyn. We came out to support a Panther who was arrested on gun charges. Thirty cops started pushing and shoving us in the hallway near the elevator. We started swinging and pushing back. I was right next to Yedwa doing my best to land a few haymakers and kicks. There were no arrests and the cops didn't follow us

when we jogged out of the building. "You're a crazy little nigger. You like to get down, don't you?" Yedwa said as he dabbed
blood from my nose with his bandanna.

"Yeah," I answered, trying to sound tough even though
I was still shaken from the fight. From that moment on, he
seemed to take a special interest in me.

One night we were sitting in a Harlem greasy spoon known
as a Jap joint. Greasy spoons are small restaurants where patrons can get large portions of greasy but delicious soul food
for cheap prices. Jap joints got their nickname because they
were staffed by Chinese cooks that Harlem residents incor-
rectly identified as Japanese. The trippy and fun part would
be the black waiter or waitress at the counter who took your
order in English and yelled it to the cooks in Chinese.

Yedwa and I were well into a few jokes and big plates of
ribs when two young thugs eased into the restaurant. They
took off their fedora hats, which they used to shield the pistols they pulled from their waistbands. One gun man jumped
behind the counter and cleaned out the register. The other
stood near me watching the patrons, his gun inches from
my head. I jerked nervously and turned to run out the door.
Yedwa grabbed my arm with a grip that was firm and calm-
ing. "Just keep eating your food, brother," he ordered in a
whisper. I mechanically shoved food in my mouth while the
gunmen stuffed money into a paper bag and scooted out
the door.

After a minute, one of the Chinese cooks ran into the street yelling, "Police, police. He rob us."

Yedwa kept calmly eating like we were at a beachfront resort. "That was real smooth," he commented between bites. "Now those brothers need to go downtown to a bank where the money is." Yedwa dabbed his goatee with a napkin and put five dollars on the counter to pay for our meals. "Let's split before the pigs get here." I followed Yedwa out, my body still electrified from the robbery, my mind blown at how cool Yedwa was. He was the father I never met, the big brother I never had.

There was a Che Guevara poster that hung in the front of the Panther office, with a quote from a speech that Che gave at the United Nations. "At the risk of sounding ridiculous, let me say that revolutionaries are guided by great feelings of love." Wow, I thought as I read that. The "love" thing. Pastor Lloyd talked about it in Sunday school and at NAACP Youth Council meetings. Noonie talked about it at home. Dr. King talked about it in his speeches, but love in the Black Panther office? What was that about? "It's about understanding that being a Panther is about serving the people, mind, body, and soul," Afeni would teach in political education class. "If you're here because you hate the oppressor and you don't have a deep love for the people, then you are a flawed revolutionary." Hearing these words made me feel less like I was doing Noonie wrong or letting down Pastor Lloyd or my favorite teachers at school.

Being a Panther meant that I was being a real aggressive

lover of freedom, and I took this part of the training to heart. "It's love that makes a Panther get up at five a.m. on a freezing winter morning to travel across town to serve breakfast to kids that are not their own," I would say in speeches at school and park rallies. "And it's love that will make a Panther get off the bus on the way home and stand between a cop who has his gun drawn and the black person being arrested, someone he's never met before." So I learned to smile while I was being taught to cook pancakes, change diapers, and fix broken windows. I learned to be enthusiastic about asking for donations and giving away the food and clothing that we collected. I learned how to find the energy, even when I was dead tired, to help a senior citizen across the street and up the stairs with her groceries.

Guns were around, but in a drawer or a closet, and not as constant companions to Panthers on duty. Once a week or so there would be weapons safety training and military drill with the purpose of giving young Panthers the skills needed to protect the Panther office or home in the event of an attack or police raid. There was a lot of talk in Panther literature and speeches about armed revolution, but it was made clear that the duty of a Panther was to organize and teach so that the political consciousness of the broad masses of people could be raised to the point that they were ready to engage in revolution. We were taught that the revolution could not be fought or won without the people and that if the masses were organized and unified enough that armed struggle might not even be necessary.

That being said and at least partially understood, I couldn't wait for my chance to fight and if need be to die in the people's revolution. It's what young Panthers talked about. Next to the poster of Che was a poster of Panther man-child hero Bobby Hutton, who was the first Panther to join at age fifteen and the first Panther to be killed at age seventeen.

I spent most of my time in the Panther office or engaged in Panther activities. I was a pretty good public speaker, with an ability to adapt the best lines from Rap Brown, Bobby Seale, Malcolm X, and Harlem Panther leaders and to make them sound like my own. I would be in lunchrooms and hallways of high schools around the city organizing students into Black Student Union chapters, a sister group of the Black Panther Party. Older Panther leaders like Lumumba and Afeni took notice of me, and I got promoted to section leader in charge of the youth cadre.

The more I rolled with the Panthers, the more my grades fell off. I went from As to Cs in most of my subjects. "School is irrelevant," I would shout at high school rallies. "The struggle is about making progressive change on the university of the streets."

Not only was my school work falling off, I was also slacking on my home chores. Noonie would have to remind me to take out the garbage, clean the cat litter box, and help her get the groceries home on Saturday morning. She was constantly on me about making up my bed and straightening my room. One day Noonie got tired of getting after me and decided to clean my room herself. As she was changing my sheets she noticed newspapers and magazines hidden between my mattress and box spring. This is where most normal fifteen-year-old boys hide their *Playboy* magazines, but when Noonie looked at my stash she got much more of an eyeful than pictures of nude girls. It was Black Panther literature. The artwork of cops depicted as pigs and little black schoolchildren blowing cops' brains out with guns while shouting, "Power to the people! Death to all fascist pigs!"

When I came in that night, Noonie had my Panther papers, her Bible, and a belt all spread out on the kitchen table, looking like it was an altar prepared for some secret society initiation. "Hi, Noonie," I said as I headed for the refrigerator. I stopped in my tracks when I saw the "altar."

"Boy, what is this?" Noonie demanded.

"What is what?" I replied, trying to play dumb.

"All of this. These books about killing cops and hating everybody I found in your room."

"You were going through my stuff?" I said indignantly.

"Don't even try that," she said firmly. "I don't know whether to bless you with this belt or kill you with this Bible, but you better tell me where this nonsense came from."

I admitted that I had been going to "a few" Panther meetings. The truth was I had been sneaking off to Panther meetings and activities for about four months now, making up lies about extra activities at school and the Minisink community center to cover my "missions."

I showed her the Ten-Point Program and tried to explain that their intention wasn't much different from what she and Pa Baltimore had espoused as part of Marcus Garvey's movement when they were young. "Oh, it's much different," Noonie said. "Mr. Garvey did not preach about hate and guns. And you are not going back to the Panthers ever again. I'll kill you myself before I let white folks kill you over this foolishness." With that, the Panther literature was thrown in the garbage and I was sent to my room.

Being the obedient grandson that I was, I went to the Panther office the next day anyway. My intention was to announce my forced retirement from the Black Panther Party and to let my Panther comrades know that I was still part of the movement in spirit and, whenever possible, in deed. "My grandmother is tripping," I said to Afeni, Lumumba, and Yedwa in front of the Panther office. "She's an Uncle Tom."

Afeni practically leaped in my chest. "Don't you dare talk about your grandmother that way," Afeni snapped. "She's just trying to love you and protect you best way she knows how."

I apologized, realizing that there was a line about elders in the community that not even the Panthers would cross.

"Yedwa, you're his section leader," Lumumba said. "Why don't you talk to his grandmother?"

"Yeah, that's cool. That'll work," Yedwa said with a smile. "I'm gonna come by your house and rap to your grandma."

It took a lot of pleading and a few days of doing extra chores around the house to convince Noonie to let Yedwa come by. "You can bring whoever you want to bring," Noonie finally said, "but I've already spoken to the Lord about this and my mind is made up."

That evening Yedwa showed up to our apartment wearing a leather jacket but without his usual array of Panther buttons. He even had on a shirt and tie. A shirt and tie? I thought. I didn't even think we were allowed to wear a shirt and tie in the Panthers.

Noonie sat in her favorite chair. Yedwa and I sat on the couch across from her. I was nervous, knees shaking like a man about to go on trial for his life. For the last four months I had walked, talked, and acted like a young badass revolutionary man. Now Noonie was about to sentence me to being a boy again. It was all up to my section leader, mentor, and hero Yedwa. "It's a pleasure to meet you, Mother Baltimore. If I didn't know better I would think you were Jamal's—excuse me, Eddie's—older sister."

"Yes, his much older sister," Noonie said, smiling slightly.

Yedwa got some points off the bat, not because of the attempted beauty compliment but because he referred to Noonie as Mother Baltimore, a term of respect that Noonie had earned in our church for being a senior congregant and the head of the missionary board.

"Mother Baltimore," Yedwa continued, "if you say Jamal—excuse me, I mean Eddie—can't come back to the Black Panther office I have to respect that cuz you're his grandmother and you're my elder."

I winced at the fact that Yedwa was using my slave name Eddie, instead of Jamal. "But ma'am," he continued, "I know that Eddie is giving you a hard time and if it's all right with you I still would like to keep an eye on him." Noonie looked intrigued. I was confused. Why was Yedwa giving up the fight so easily, and what was this stuff about keeping an eye on me? "Ma'am, if you set his curfew for nine o'clock and he is not in the house by eight forty-five I will take off this garrison belt buckle and I'll whip his butt."

By then I was really unsure. What the hell was Yedwa talking about? He was supposed to tell Noonie that I'm a revolutionary and that I need to come and go as I please. "Ma'am, I know Eddie can be doing a lot better in school. If you want him to bring you an eighty on his next math test and he doesn't bring you a ninety, I will take these size fifteen combat boots and I'll give him a swift kick in the rear." At this point I was trying desperately to catch Yedwa's attention. He was making things worse. Yedwa never looked my way. He kept a humble gaze on Noonie.

Noonie nodded her head slowly, leaning back in her chair for a moment. She glanced up at the heavens as she checked in with the Lord. "You know my mind is pretty made up about this," Noonie said. "Eddie doesn't have a father and it's really hard raising a teenage boy alone. But if you're going to look after him like you said, and make sure that he does better in school, that when he comes in the house he obeys my rules, then he can come by the Panthers a couple of times a week."

I could barely believe what I was hearing. Yedwa had just moved a mountain and parted the Red Sea. This was unprecedented. From the time she started taking care of me when I was four to this very moment, Noonie never changed her mind about a punishment decision.

Yedwa stayed for dinner. After home-baked apple pie and hot chocolate, he hugged Noonie like she was his grandmother. Noonie let me go outside to take out the trash and to chat with Yedwa. "That was cool, brother," I said admiringly, "the way you laid it down with Noonie was really something."

"Well, in case you didn't realize it, I was dead serious. You need to do better in school and you need to stop worrying this woman or I'm gonna be getting in your ass. In the Panther Party we say that we are motivated by our undying love for the people. Isn't your grandmother part of the people?" Yedwa turned and walked away. I watched him for a few minutes and headed back to our apartment. When I got inside I hugged Noonie and told her that I loved her. For the first time in many tumultuous adolescent months I really meant it.

5

Busted with the Big Cats

April 1, 1969. It was a Thursday night and there was a big rally for the Harlem Five at a public school there. The Harlem Five was a group of five young black men who were community organizers in the Lincoln projects in the heart of Harlem. Hannibal, Sayid, Wallace, David, and Mustafa were college students and community counselors who preached black nationalism in the spirit of Malcolm X.

They worked with tenants organizing rent strikes, and they set up after-school programs where kids did homework and learned black history and the martial arts. Because of their efforts, gang violence and drug dealing was reduced to almost zero in the projects. But in 1968 they were arrested and jailed for conspiracy to declare war on the cops. Many people in the community felt they had been framed, and on that April Fool's night the school auditorium was packed with their supporters. The Panthers had worked side by side with the Harlem Five on tenants' rights issues, community safety patrols designed to protect the elderly, and efforts to get to get rid of drugs in the neighborhood. Members of the Harlem Tenants Council, the Republic of New Africa, the Revolutionary Action Movement, and the Black Student Union, along with parents, grandmothers, and neighbors from the projects, were all part of the standing-room-only crowd.

That night's gathering was more than a political rally—it was a cultural event. There were African dancers, a jazz quartet, and a concert by the Last Poets, a group said by many to have invented rap. Their lyrics and poems performed over jazz riffs, bass licks, and African drum beats were both incendiary and highly entertaining. The men in the group, Felipe, Abiodun, Kain, and Yusef, were stars of the black movement.

I had heard of the Last Poets, but this was my first time seeing them perform. Since I was sitting with the Black Panther contingent, I had a front-row seat.

The Last Poets were awesome, and listening to their rap poems like "New York, New York" and "When the Revolution

Comes" made me feel not only revolutionary but so damn cool. In between the acts, various speakers took the stage to talk about the plight of the Harlem Five. None was more powerful than Lumumba Shakur, the captain and the leader of the Harlem and Bronx branches of the Black Panther Party. "In order to get the Harlem Five back on the streets, brothers and sisters, we may have to take it to the streets. Frederick Douglass said, 'Power only concedes to power.' But we have to take the power of the people to the courtrooms, and if they don't free these brothers, we have to take the courthouse down." We all cheered and pumped our fists while chanting, "Power to the people. Free the Harlem Five!"

After the rally, a group of fifty Panthers stood in military formation outside the school. I was now a section leader and stood in front of a group of fifteen young Panthers from the Bronx.

Captain Lumumba walked up and inspected our formation. "Looking good, brothers and sisters," he said. "You're dismissed." Then Lumumba waved me over and asked me if I could open the Harlem Panther office on the way to school the next day.

I stuck my chest out and said, "Of course." He smiled, handed me the keys, and walked off.

This was a great honor, I thought, to be given the trust and responsibility of opening the office. What Lumumba didn't know was that my school was in the Bronx. There was no way I would make it to school on time. What the hell? Playing hooky for the revolution and the Panthers seemed like an easy choice.

By the time I got off my subway stop in the Bronx and jogged home, it was past midnight. I tiptoed in the house and almost made it to my room. Then Noonie opened her bedroom door. "Why you coming in the house so late?"

"There was a big rally and then the trains were running late. I didn't want to call and wake you up." The excuses streamed out.

Noonie shook her head. "You think I can sleep when you're out running the streets?"

"I wasn't in the street. I told you I was at a rally."

But Noonie was too frustrated to care about rallies versus streets. "Keep messing up. You hear me? Keep messing up." And with that she closed her door. I knew I was on thin ice, but I decided to let the situation be. I took a quick shower, slipped on my pajamas, and climbed in bed.

It seemed like I had just closed my eyes when I realized Noonie was shaking me. "What? Okay. I'm getting up. I'm going to school," I said groggily as I hopped up.

"There's somebody banging on the door," she said. "It's four o'clock in the morning." As my head cleared I heard the doorbell ringing and the sound of pounding on the front door.

"There's a gas leak!" a man's voice roared from the other side of the door.

"All right, I'm coming," I yelled as I descended the flight of stairs that led to the door.

"Gas leak," the muffled voice said again.

I pulled up my droopy pajama bottoms and peered through the peephole. There were a dozen or more cops standing there with rifles, shotguns, and bulletproof vests. I stumbled back in shock like someone kicked the air out of my stomach. "There's no gas leak in here," I said. My adrenaline was pumping as I turned to head back up the stairs. My thoughts raced: Get dressed, you're half naked and vulnerable. Get to your grandmother and protect her, make a phone call to the Panthers for help, dive out of the second-story back window and run!

The door flew off the hinges as I reached the third step. Cops in SWAT gear tackled me and threw me against the wall. I was blinded by the glare of flashlight they shone in my eyes.

"Eddie Joseph, you're under arrest," a cop shouted.

"My name is Jamal," I replied through clenched teeth.

"That's all right," the cop sneered. "We got a warrant for him too." They clamped on a pair of handcuffs so tightly that they started cutting into my wrists.

Noonie peered over the top of the staircase. "What's going on?" she demanded. "What are you doing to my son?"

"He's under arrest," a detective snapped, "and you stay back!"

"Watch how you talk to my grandmother!" The anxiety

I felt for myself was superseded by the protective love I felt for Noonie. I lurched toward the detective. The other cops instantly slammed me back into the wall.

"I'm all right, son," Noonie shouted. "Don't fight them." I looked up at Noonie. I could tell she was upset and confused, but her voice and eyes were calm. It helped me to cool down.

The cops took me upstairs to my room and held me at gunpoint while they let me put on a pair of pants and a sweater over my pajamas. Then they recuffed me and asked, "Where are the bombs and the guns?" I knew from the legal-aid classes I took in the Panthers that when dealing with the cops I shouldn't make any statements, so I said nothing.

They began turning my room upside down. They found a .32-caliber revolver and a military training manual. This made them tear shit up even more. Then they yanked my Order of the Feather sweater from the closet, threw it on the ground, and stepped on it. Besides my Panther beret, the sweater was one of my prized possessions. "Don't step on my sweater, motherfucker," I said, lurching forward. Again, I was roughly restrained.

"Get him out of here," the detective barked.

"Call the Panther office, Noonie," I said as the cops whisked me by her. "Ask for Dhoruba or Lumumba. They'll get me out."

Dawn was breaking as I was led onto the street in handcuffs. I stopped in my tracks when I saw a dozen cop cars lined up in front of the building. More cops with rifles and combat gear stood poised to attack. My heart fluttered. They're ready to kill me, I thought. If I had leaped out a window, they would have gunned me down like a dog. The cops shoved me along and placed me in the backseat of an unmarked detective car. Detectives sat on either side of me.

An older detective showed me pictures of various Panthers. First Lumumba Shakur. "Do you know him?"

"No," I replied.

Next they showed me a photo of Afeni Shakur. "Do you know her?"

"No," I mumbled.

Then they showed me a mug shot of Eldridge Cleaver. "Do you know him?"

"No."

The detective pointed at Eldridge. "You don't know Eldridge Cleaver, minister of information of the Black Panther Party?" Now I said nothing.

The detective closed his photo folder and spoke to the uniformed cop behind the wheel. "Let's go." The car pulled out.

I just looked out the window as we raced through the streets, sirens blasting—cop cars in front of and behind us. I was a little shook up, but I was proud too. Being arrested at sixteen or any age for being a Panther was a mark of honor. It meant that you had become enough of a thorn in the system's side for them to come after you. Typically, it would be a gun charge, disorderly conduct, or a trumped-up robbery charge. You would stay in jail for a few days or a month while the Black Panther Party raised your bail. Then you would come out to a hero's welcome at the Panther office. Brothers and sisters would applaud and embrace you. You would give a little "struggle continues" speech and then go to a reception at someone's house complete with home cooked food, Motown on the stereo, and dancing into the wee hours.

As we pulled up to the Tombs (the Manhattan House of Detention), I wondered what I had done to grab the pigs' attention. Maybe I was being charged with inciting a riot for the Eldridge Cleaver/Rap Brown cloned speech I gave in a high school assembly one day. I got suspended from school for two days after calling the principal a fascist swine. Maybe he reported me to the police. Maybe one of the Uncle Tom students told them about the time my .32 revolver slipped out of my book bag and fell to the floor during the Black Student Association meeting. I took it as a cue to recite a Panther quote: "An unarmed people are subject to slavery at any time" and sheepishly picked up the pistol and put it away. The Panthers lent me the gun because I had received death threats on the phone and in the mail. *We're gonna shoot, lynch, and burn your little Black Panther nigger ass,* one note read, *and then we're gonna kill that black bitch grandmother of yours.*

Maybe it was because I was a section leader now, which

was the Panthers' equivalent of being a sergeant. The *senior* Panthers (the ones who were pushing twenty-four) had taken a real liking to me. I had the responsibility of running the youth cadre (the twenty or so other Panthers in high school), and I was now helping to teach some of the political education classes and technical equipment classes, including military drill, basic hand-to-hand combat, and weapon safety. Once or twice a month there was a rally or a big "central" staff meeting where several hundred Panthers from around the city got together, usually in the auditorium of the Long Island University campus in Brooklyn. Now that I had been arrested, I would be asked to stand and speak at the next central staff meeting. I might even get a Panther girlfriend out of this.

The cops led me to the Manhattan DA's office. When they walked me into the squad room I saw Brother Dhoruba, one of the top leaders of the New York Panthers. I was overjoyed and impressed. He must have gotten Noonie's call and dashed down to get me out.

"Right on, brother," I said as I gave the black-power salute. "You made it down here already."

"Very funny," Dhoruba replied as he gave the cop standing next to him his other hand to fingerprint. It hit me then that Dhoruba was under arrest too.

Then I looked around and saw a dozen other key New York Panthers in handcuffs or in holding cells. Lumumba Shakur and his wife, Afeni; Joan Bird (a nineteen-year-old nursing student who had been arrested and severely beaten by cops two months earlier); Bob Collier; Dr. Curtis Powell (who had a PhD in biochemistry); Clark Squire (a computer expert); Baba Odinga; Ali Bey Hassan; and the youngest Panther (next to myself), Katara, a high school senior.

The mood was almost festive with the Panthers shouting greetings to one another and taunts at the police. "This ain't nothing but pig harassment," Dhoruba told a detective once we were all placed in a huge holding cell. "Our lawyers are going to have a field day with you." Everyone seemed confident that this was a giant sweep meant to shake up the New York chapter. "We'll all be out by the weekend," said Lumumba. He should know, I thought. He's already out on bail on three other Panther-related cases.

From my cell I thought I caught a glimpse of Yedwa and of a quiet Panther named Gene Roberts. Gene was his usual quiet, almost mournful, self. Gene was a navy veteran who was a member of the security section. He taught me about handguns and standing post should I ever be given body-guard detail. We passed the time doing push-ups and joking about the different ploys the cops used to get into our respective homes. Some of the SWAT teams yelled "Fire." Others used the same gas leak line that was tried on me.

Then we were handcuffed, surrounded by cops, and walked through the dark maze of corridors and barred gates that led to the courthouse. We were placed in another large holding cell, and they started taking the others away one by one. I didn't see anyone return. I wondered, as our numbers dwindled, if they were taking us out to be shot. Finally they came for me. I was led into a courtroom that was filled with Panthers, supporters, cops, court guards, and lawyers. An older man with long hair walked over to me and shook my hand. "Hi, I'm Bill Kunstler. I'm your lawyer." The cops guided me to the defense table. Bill Kunstler and a young lawyer named Gerald Lefcourt stood on either side of me.

The court clerk began reading from a paper: "The People versus Lumumba Shakur et al. The defendant Eddie Joseph, also known as Jamal Baltimore, is charged with conspiracy to commit murder, conspiracy to commit arson, and attempted murder. How do you plead?"

"What?" was all my confused brain and shocked mouth could blurt out.

"The defendant pleads not guilty," Kunstler said.

"Bail is set in the amount of one hundred thousand dollars," the judge said.

"What?" I repeated. The number staggered me. Noonie and I had never even seen a thousand dollars.

"Judge, this is the defendant's first arrest. He is an honor student, has strong ties in the community, and is barely sixteen. He should not be charged as an adult . . ."

The judge cut Kunstler off: "Bail is one hundred thousand dollars. Remand the defendant."

"Power to the people, Brother Jamal!" someone shouted as I was led from the courtroom. I reflexively raised my first in the black-power salute and shouted, "Power!" The supporters began applauding. I caught a glimpse of Noonie in the third row, looking very sad. "Noonie," I called out, "Ma!" But my voice was drowned out by the clapping, revolutionary slogans, and the judge banging his gavel for order. Noonie waved back as two burly court guards escorted me from the courtroom.

The court guards placed me in a small holding cell. I had expected to be reunited with the other Panthers, but the guards had other plans. A few minutes later the guards put Katara in the cell with me. "What's happening? Why aren't we with the other Panthers?" we demanded of the guards. The guards ignored us except for a black guard who eventually informed us that because we were under twenty-one we were being taken to Rikers Island.

A few hours later a contingent of guards and cops shackled us and led us to a paddy wagon. It was built low and wide like an armored car. The prisoner compartment was like a tomb: metal benches along the wall for seating, tiny barred slits for windows. The paddy wagon pulled off, escorted by two police cars. There were no seat belts and every time we hit a bump, Katara and I would bounce around like jumping beans, sometimes banging our heads on the ceiling or winding up on the floor. Since we were shackled we would have to roll and shimmy around the paddy wagon in order to get back to the bench.

It was around midnight when we got to Rikers. A team of guards took us from the van to holding cells. Katara and I were strip-searched and led to isolation cells, also known as the hole or the bing in different cell blocks. My cell was cramped and dirty, with a paper-thin mattress on a metal slab passing for a bed. My only bedding was a coarse gray blanket. Mice darted around the floor looking for food like shoppers at a mall. When I stomped and yelled, they would dart into holes in the concrete, and then reappear moments later. This was obviously their jail and I was the visitor.

Fighting my fear, fists clenched, I stared at the single light-bulb hanging in its metal enclosure. "I'm a Panther," I repeated aloud. "Pigs can't break me." Then I recited the Ten-Point Program. "We want freedom. We want the power to determine the destiny of our black community." The guards turned the cell light out. I started thinking about Noonie, wondering if she was okay. Then I pretended I was in the bunk at Camp Minisink, which finally relaxed me enough to fall asleep.

6

To the Belly of the Beast

Even though it was a city jail, as opposed to a state or federal prison, Rikers Island, or "the Rock," as it was known by inmates and guards, was a hard place to do time. Part penitentiary, part gladiator school. A person doing time on the Rock quickly found out that you had to be strong to survive.

The next morning the guard opened my cell and a young black prisoner handed me a breakfast tray. Watery powdered milk, a box of generic corn flakes, four slices of white bread, and a cup of coffee that tasted like brown dishwater. Later the guard let me out of my cell for a shower. Two more meals were brought to me: a bologna sandwich with tea, and a rubbery greenish piece of meat that was supposed to be liver. I ate what I could and did push-ups to keep my strength up. Every time the guard opened my cell to leave a food tray, I jumped to my feet expecting to hear him say, "You've been released." But each time an inmate would just pass me a food tray and the door would shut.

A black prisoner named Merciful Allah passed by my cell using a heavy industrial mop to clean the floor. He was part of the "house gang," a small group of inmates selected by the guards to do custodial and light maintenance work in the cell block. Merciful lived in Three Block but was escorted over to the "seg" unit twice a day to do chores. Merciful would finish cleaning the corridor and then stop by my cell to talk for a few minutes until the guard chased him away.

He told me my arrest was all over the news. Merciful slipped me a newspaper that had pictures of everyone who had been arrested and indicted. The police were reportedly saying that twenty-one Black Panthers were set to go to war with the government. District Attorney Frank Hogan said that we were arrested days, perhaps hours, before we were going to plant bombs in major department stores at the height of the Easter shopping season. We were also accused of planning to bomb the Bronx Botanical Gardens as well as police stations, where we would be shooting cops as they fled the explosion. I stared at my mug shot in the paper, trying to process the allegations and comprehend my surroundings.

Merciful's real name was Tony Mason. He had a scar on his right cheek, running from his ear to his mouth, and an Islamic star and crescent tattoo on his arm. He took the name Merciful after joining a group known as the Five Percenters, which believed that the black man was God, and all of the members took the last name Allah.

Merciful was twenty years old and was about to "go upstate" to a maximum-security prison to serve five years for sticking up a liquor store. This was Merciful's third bid. He had done two years in a youth house and three years in Elmira Reformatory for burglary and robbery. Damn, I thought, twenty years old and he's already spent a quarter of his life in prison.

I would talk to Merciful about prison being a concentration camp that was part of a military-industrial complex designed to exploit and enslave black men for the purpose of profit. Merciful would talk about the black man being God and white man being the devil.

He would hand me a cigarette and ask a bunch of questions about the Panthers. Real cigarettes were like gold in prison. In fact, cigarettes were used as currency and also for gambling. Prisoners would shoot dice, play cards, and bet on basketball games and boxing matches with cigarettes. "Juggling" was a big loan-shark business in jail. "Jugglers" would walk through the cell block calling out "Two for one" or "Three for one."

This meant that you could get a pack of cigarettes (or cookies, deodorant, or toothpaste) today with the understanding that you would pay back two or three packs on commissary day.

Many of the jugglers were also part of the house gang. The house gang got to stay out when the rest of the inmates were locked in their cells for the afternoon count and evening lockup. This meant they could pursue their juggling enterprise as they moved around the tiers, waxing, mopping, handing out clean sheets, and bringing food trays to inmates who were locked down in segregation for security or medical reasons.

Merciful was part of the house gang and a juggler, but he never asked for anything back when he gave me a few cigarettes, real toothpaste (not the tin of tooth powder inmates were usually given), or a sandwich. He was just fascinated to meet a "real Black Panther" and was amazed that I appeared to be "so soft" compared with the "hard niggers" he imagined the Panthers to be.

He asked if the Panthers were coming to break me out. I told him that the charges against us were all trumped up and that the lawyers were working to get the case dismissed. He warned me not to trust anyone because the jail was filled with snitches and "booty bandits." Booty bandits were prisoners who liked to rape "new jacks"—new guys like myself.

The truth is I was secretly hoping that a Panther commando squad would blow down the walls of the cell block and free me. I hated jail. The metal walls of the tiny cell seemed like they were closing in on me. I felt like I was losing my mind. I inspected myself in the metal mirror. I looked like a crazy man. My Afro was matted and wild. My T-shirt was dirty. My eyes were puffy with depression and anxiety. Merciful passed me a plastic Afro comb. "Stash that in your mattress," he said. "The guards consider that contraband." I picked out my Afro, then used the comb to tear a slit in my mattress and hid it. Merciful also gave me a clean pair of socks, drawers, and a T-shirt. He told me how to stop up my sink with toilet paper so I could fill it with cold water and use the prison soap to lather up and wash my dirty clothes.

There were other prisoners in segregation. Most were inmates who were serving three to thirty days for fighting, disobeying an order, or possessing contraband. A few were mentally disturbed inmates who were waiting for beds to open up in Bellevue's prison psych ward. The rest were labeled snitches—inmates who were being held in protective custody because they were testifying against their codefendants or other inmates.

A few days after I arrived at Rikers, three guards came to my cell. The cell door rolled open. I stood, uncertain as to why the guards were there. "You have a visitor," one of the guards said. I cautiously stepped outside my cell. They escorted me to the visiting room. Two dozen inmates sat on stools and talked into telephone receivers to their relatives who sat on the other side of the Plexiglas windows. I was considered a high security risk, so the guards led me past the other inmates and locked me into a small corner metal booth. The inside of the booth felt like a coffin. I dripped sweat and took slow deep breaths to keep from passing out.

A few minutes later a guard led Noonie to a chair on the other side of the Plexiglas. She looked frail and bewildered in this concentration-camp-like environment, but I was happy to see her. Noonie smiled and started talking. I picked up my telephone receiver and gestured to her to do the same. The damn phones didn't work. I banged on my cubicle wall, yelling for a guard. I motioned to Noonie to call for the guard on her side of the Plexiglas. She shook her head no and mouthed, "Let's not make trouble."

"We're not making trouble, Noonie," I yelled. "I have a legal right to a visit. These phones are supposed to work. They're treating me like an animal in here." I pounded the cubicle wall. I saw tears forming in Noonie's eyes and calmed myself down.

I located a small mesh covered vent below the Plexiglas window where I could shout to Noonie and place my ear to hear her response.

"Are you okay?" I yelled.

"I'm fine, sweetheart," Noonie replied, "but I'm worried about you."

"I'm fine. Don't worry about me. This is just all a bunch of harassment. The lawyers will have us out soon. Did anybody from the party call you?"

"Somebody called," Noonie said. "But I told them I didn't have anything to say." My heart sank as I pictured Noonie hanging up on a Panther leader.

"But if they were from the Panthers, they were trying to help. Maybe they had information from the lawyers."

Noonie set her jaw like a strong African mask. "That Black Panther mess put you here. Now they want to help?"

When Noonie got like this, there was no reasoning with her, so I left the subject of phone calls alone. She told me that Reverend Lloyd and the whole church were praying for me. I wanted to say, "Praise the Lord and pass the ammunition," but I knew Noonie would have found a way to slap me through the Plexiglas window. I just nodded my head and mouthed the words, "Thank you."

The guard came for Noonie and told her the visit was over. "Over? Visits are supposed to be thirty minutes. My mother's only been here for ten," I yelled at the guard through the vent. "The phone doesn't work *and* you're cutting my visit short?" The guard ignored me. Noonie told me she loved me, blew me a kiss, and left. The guards left me in the visiting coffin for another hour. When they finally let me out I was drenched, weak, dehydrated, and pissed.

Merciful was sitting in one of the regular visiting cubicles waiting for his visitor to arrive. "Peace, black man," he said, and smiled. "You have a good visit with your people?"

"Naw, man," I snapped, "these pigs messed with my whole visit."

One of the guards escorting me was a short, stocky black dude. He spun around, jabbed his finger in my chest, and got nose to nose with me like a boxer before the first bell. "I ain't gonna be all them damn pigs," he spit.

"You don't have to be one if you don't act like one," I replied almost politely.

The guard jabbed me with his finger again. "I said I ain't gonna be all them damn pigs."

I knew the next words were going to get me in trouble, but I was too mad to hold back. "I'm sorry. I meant to say these motherfucking pigs are messing with my visit."

The guard was holding his prison key ring, which he used to deliver a hard smack against the side of my head. I staggered back. He came at me with a punch. I managed to partially block it and landed a kick in his fat belly. I was aiming for his balls, but it was enough to wobble him back. Then two white guards jumped on me and started pounding away with punches. Prison guards don't actually carry clubs for fear that inmates will snatch them and use them as weapons against them. It's the riot squad, or "goon squad," that wears helmets and uses clubs, shields, and tear gas to overpower prisoners.

Since the visiting corridor is narrow, the guards had a hard time subduing me. We banged up against the wall, trading blows until they were able to drag me to the main corridor. Once there I dropped to the ground and curled into a protective ball the way I had been trained in Panther self-defense classes. The guards handcuffed me. There were a number of inmates and guards and a black captain named Woods in the main corridor. With all the witnesses, the beating stopped. The captain told them to take me back to "seg" and write up an incident report. Captain Woods had a reputation for being hard but fair. He did not allow guards to use "excessive force" on his watch.

Captain Woods shadowed the guards as they took me back to my cell and locked me in. He asked me what happened. I told him about being locked in the broken cubicle and making a general statement about the pigs. He asked me who threw the first blow. I showed him the swelling that the key ring left near my eye. Captain Woods just nodded and walked away. I slept with one eye open, expecting the guards to return in larger numbers with a beat-down.

My first week in prison felt like a year, but I knew Noonie's trek from Rikers Island back to her apartment in the North Bronx must have felt like an eternity. There were locked gates to go through, a long wait for the bus to take her off Rikers Island, then another bus to the subway station, followed by a series of trains on the two-hour ride home. Eventually, I convinced her to visit only once each month.

I would write Noonie letters assuring here that I was doing fine and that the lawyers were making progress with the case. She would send me shorter notes with encouraging Bible quotes and well wishes from church members. It was hard to talk about the Panther 21 case with Noonie. She understood and seemed to agree that it was a frame-up, but she still felt that I had gotten mixed up with the "wrong people," while believing that the judge would let me go because it was my first mistake.

The day after my scuffle with the visiting room guard, Captain Woods came to my cell with another officer. "Pack your stuff up, Mr. Joseph," he said. "You're being transferred."

"Where?" I asked.

"Three Block," he said. "General population."

This is weird, I thought. I get into a fight with three guards and actually get released from segregation? I wondered if this might be a set-up, but I rolled up my few possessions in my blanket and followed Captain Woods. As we walked down the main corridor, Captain Woods explained that the black guard who hit me had been transferred to a different unit on Rikers. "I don't like my guards hitting inmates with key rings," he said, "but you ain't gonna get very far calling my guards pigs either."

I accepted this as compromise justice and stepped into Three Block. My new home.

7

Walk Slow and Drink Plenty of Cold Water

I walked down the "flats" (the ground floor) and up the stairs to my assigned cell on the third tier. The cell block was huge. Four tiers with two inmates per cell. Four hundred adolescents with hormones raging and anger and frustration pulsing through their veins. The charges ranged from burglary and drug possession to armed robbery and murder. All of the teenagers in this section of Rikers were trial prisoners. They either could not afford bail or had been remanded without bail. It was sad to see young men locked up for relatively minor offenses because their family couldn't afford a few hundred dollars to get them out, but that was the case for a lot of the young inmates at Rikers.

There was a hierarchy of respect related to what you were charged with. Murder and armed robbery were on the high end. Burglary and grand larceny auto were on the low end and considered to be "meatball" cases. Because I was facing so much time (three-hundred-plus years), and because my indictment listed charges that included attempted murder of police officers and arson, I was considered among the heavies. But as Merciful put it, I "looked soft," skinny and light-complexioned with a curly Afro. When I walked down the flats, the other inmates would stare at me and whisper. Many of them were wondering how a choirboy-looking dude like me could be hooked up with the Black Panthers.

My cell partner was a nineteen-year-old Puerto Rican guy named Manny, who looked more like a marine recruit than an inmate. Compact physique, buzz-cut hair, and sporting a heart shaped tattoo that said MARIA. He had done two and a half years in Elmira Reformatory and was really angry at himself for catching a new three-year sentence for armed robbery. Manny never talked about the details of his case. He said the cell block was full of snitches who would give up their own mother in a second to get out of jail. Manny was "jail wise," meaning he knew all the ins and outs of doing time. At first he had very little to say to me except "take the top bunk and don't touch my shit," but eventually he loosened up.

The guards would make mail deliveries by placing letters on the bars after evening lockup. The envelopes would already be open, having been read and inspected for contraband. Manny asked me to read him a letter from his girlfriend, Maria. He seemed agitated and embarrassed about asking, saying that Maria liked to use "all these big fucking words." I read him the letter, then helped him write a response, much like in the play I had read about Cyrano de Bergerac. In payment, Manny handed me two packs of cigarettes and asked me to give him my word that this "letter shit" would stay between us. I told him he had my word but turned down the cigarettes.

"Knowledge is power, brother," I said as I handed his cigarettes back. "And the power should be shared by all the people."

"You a strange dude," Manny decided as he looked me up and down, "but you all right. I'm gonna teach you how to jail.

"Walk slow and drink plenty of cold water," Manny advised. "That's what an old black dude taught me when I first got upstate. That means think two or three times before you make any moves, and drink lots of water to keep your kidneys clean. There's all kinds of hepatitis and other bullshit going around in the joint."

Manny taught me that the cell desk could be used as a stove to make quick dishes like grilled cheese, fried salami, eggs, and even French toast. The secret to not getting caught by the guards was to grill quickly and to do it after they had made a big count or a shakedown in the hopes that they were just too tired to climb stairs and search the cell block for an errant griller.

The cell toilet could be used as a refrigerator. The inmates would soap it up, scrub it clean, flush it a few times to get the water ice cold, and drop in tiny sealed cartons of milk or plastic sealed packets of salami and other meat to keep it cold. If you had to go to the bathroom, you took the items out, did your business, scrubbed the toilet, and turned it back into a refrigerator. Clothes could get a hot-water wash by taking them with you to the showers; pressing was accomplished by laying them out under your mattress before turning in for the night.

At night, after lock-in, inmates would throw empty cookie boxes attached to thin ropes made from braided sheets out of their cells, running them either down the tier or over the railing. This technique was called running a line. The intent was to get your cookie box to your homeboy in another part of the cell block so that you could pass or receive some snacks, a few cigarettes, a "kite" (a letter), or drugs. Many fights and stabbings happened because someone intercepted a line and stole the goods or because an inmate refused to get out of bed or off the toilet to pass a line that landed in front of his cell.

Torn strips of prison sheets could also be braided into thick rope. This "Rikers rope" was used in escapes and suicides:

Witness one kid, a seventeen-year-old black inmate named Teddy, who wandered around the cell block looking like a homeless guy. It was clear that Teddy needed some counseling and medical attention, so I went to the guards and they told me that it was really none of my business, but he was on the list for a transfer to Bellevue. That night Teddy used Rikers rope to hang himself from the light box in his cell.

We saw Teddy's hanging body as we marched down the tier for breakfast. Neck swollen, eyes bulging, saliva drooling from enlarged purple lips. "Yo guards, a hangup on Three Tier. Hangup!" Manny yelled. "Hangup" was slang for a hanging, and the guards came running. Manny and I grabbed Teddy's legs and lifted his body while a guard cut the rope. We laid him on the floor. Other guards arrived and yanked us out of the way even though we were trying to help. "Shit. He's dead," one of the guards shouted as he checked Teddy's pulse. A siren buzzed and lock-down orders came through the loudspeaker. The doors of our cells rolled shut as the guards carried Teddy's body out on a stretcher.

Inmates called out to each other from their cells saying that Teddy hung himself because he had gotten two years for grand larceny auto and was scared to go upstate to do his bid. Others said he was tired of being pressed by the booty bandits. I had seen Teddy go into the shower room with some of the guys from the house gang; now I realized they were taking him there to have sex.

An hour after they had discovered Teddy's suicide, the goon squad came to shake down the cell block. There was a symphony of running water as inmates flushed their lines, Rikers rope, and other contraband before the goon squad could get to their cells.

There were numerous places around the cell to stash contraband items, including street money, drugs, and weapons. Air vents, lighting fixtures, and bunk-bed legs could all hold items that had been epoxyed with toothpaste and camouflaged with paint made from tooth powder and cigarette ashes.

Manny showed me his weapons stash, which consisted of two homemade knives called shanks, figas, or figs. A figa was a piece of a jailhouse mattress spring that had been straightened, filed into an ice-pick tip, and crowned with a handle made from a sheet or a blanket. It was a wicked-looking weapon that could easily puncture the body and inflict major damage. Manny also knew how to fashion bedsprings into brass knuckles. Rikers was known as a gladiator school, and it appeared I was celling with a master blacksmith.

Manny had very little to say to me outside the cell. He was a loner who didn't hang out with anybody. "I just want to do my bid and get the fuck out of here and back to my girl and my baby daughter." Most other inmates would hang out in different groups on the flats—the Thugs; the Five Percenters; the Latin Brothers; and the Workout Kids, who did a thousand sit-ups and push-ups a day.

Three times a day a guard's voice would blare through the loudspeaker system ordering us to line up for chow. We would march in two lines down the corridor to the mess hall where inmates could briefly mingle with their homeboys and codefendants in the other cell blocks. Our only utensil was a spoon, which worked fine for the watery oatmeal but was challenging on the rubbery meats and half-cooked potatoes. On the way out of the mess hall each inmate had to place his tray on the stack and his used spoon in a bucket, all overseen by several guards.

One night I came back from the mess hall to find a box of cookies and a couple of packs of cigarettes on my bunk. I thought they were intended for Manny, left on my bunk by mistake. He occasionally made figas or knuckles for one of his Latino homeboys and got paid with commissary. "Yo, Manny, I think somebody left these for you," I said, pointing to the commissary.

"That's for you," he nodded. "That dude, Lefty, from the house gang, left that shit."

Lefty was a muscle-bound, cross-eyed black inmate who was captain of the house gang. He was a bully with a devastating left hook that he used to knock out inmates he had a beef with. Lefty and Merciful and a few other inmates would sometimes come around to talk to me about the Panthers. I even started a small PE class where I would explain the Ten-Point Program and other aspects of Panther ideology. Lefty would listen, watch me intently, and walk away. I knew Lefty was a big-time juggler and thought he was offering me some commissary credit. Manny straightened me out, explaining that Lefty was a notorious booty bandit who was trying to gift me before he set me up to take my "manhood" (the Rikers term for being seduced or raped).

A wave of shock, anger, and fear rolled through me as I jumped to my feet. "Take my manhood," I said. "I don't hang out with that dude." I had been taking Manny's advice and keeping to myself, mostly doing calisthenics and reading, except when guys came up to me to talk about the Panthers.

"That don't matter to a snake like Lefty," Manny replied. "In fact, half those dudes that are coming up to talk to you are plottin' on ways to get you alone so they can jump you. And your boy Merciful is down with them."

Manny could see that I was reeling, trying to figure it all out. "This shit ain't really none of my business," he said quietly, "but the only way to back a dude like Lefty off of you is to sneak up on him with a mop ringer or a figa and fuck him up real good in front of everybody. And while he's on the ground bleedin' you yell at that motherfucker so that everybody can hear you, 'I'm a man, motherfucker. I ain't nobody's bitch, motherfucker. Anybody try to take my manhood is getting wasted.' The guards are gonna fuck you up and put you in the bing for a couple of months, but when you come out the dudes is gonna know that you ain't to be fucked with."

The guards turned the cell lights out and Manny hopped

into his bunk. "You can use one of the figas if you want to—just let me know so I can get rid of the rest of my shit when they lock you up and come to shake the cell down." With that he rolled over and fell asleep. I stood staring into the cell block night. For the first time since I was arrested I realized that I was alone. My fellow adolescent Panther Katara was in another unit. And my other Panther comrades were in different jails. Whatever reputation the Black Panther Party had as an organization wasn't going to protect me from the young gladiators in the Riker coliseum.

I tried to picture myself splitting Lefty's head open with a mop ring, or jabbing him in the lower back with a figa. I saw a fig do a lot of damage when two Latino jugglers jumped on a white boy who failed to pay his cigarette debt. They stabbed him eight times in the blink of an eye. The white inmate ran to the front of the cell block and collapsed. The guards hit the alarm and ordered an emergency lockdown. An army of goon-squad guards shook all the cells down and the Latino jugglers were taken away in handcuffs. We heard through the grapevine that the white inmate died the next day.

I couldn't make it work in my head. I couldn't see myself attacking another prisoner, no matter who it was. That was what our captors wanted. As long as they kept us divided and fighting, we were easy to control. I joined the Panthers to fight the enemy, to battle the pigs, not to go to war with others who were oppressed just like me.

The next day I went to Lefty's cell and handed him the

cookies and cigarettes he left on my bunk. "Look, brother, I think you got the wrong idea," I said, trying to portray as much strength as I could. "I want to be cool with you, but I don't go that way."

Lefty cracked a sly smile. "I got plenty of girls on the outside. Just like you do. This is just something to do to get through this bit. Ain't nobody got to know nothin'." He stroked my cheek.

I knocked his hand away. "I'm telling you I don't play that," I barked, half settling into a fighting stance.

His face went grim. "You can't beat me, nigga. I'll take that booty if I want. It'll be shit on my dick or blood on my knife in this motherfucker."

I balled my fist ready to do my best against Lefty. I was slightly taller, but Lefty had three tough street years and twenty-five pounds of muscle on me. He stared me down for a tiny eternity and then laughed. "I'm just bullshittin'. I ain't gonna do nothin' to you. But a bunch of these other foul niggas is about to take you off. You better let me look out for you."

"Naw, that's all right," I said.

I stepped out of Lefty's cell and saw some of the dudes from the house gang hanging around. I could tell from the look in their eyes that they were checking to see if anything had gone down between Lefty and me, be it sex or violence. I walked to the back of the cell block and started doing calisthenics. A little while later, Merciful walked up and asked if I was all right. I told him I was cool and kept doing sit-ups. Merciful could tell I was angry and explained that while he wasn't part of Lefty's crew, he couldn't really get involved if Lefty was trying to press me. "I know," I replied. "I gotta handle it myself. Jailhouse law." Merciful just nodded and walked away.

There were no direct come-ons from Lefty for the next few days, but his body language and the looks he gave me were a clear sign that he was going to make a move.

Two weeks later the guards took me out of my cell to go to court. I was handcuffed and placed in the back of the "hell wagon," which drove from Rikers Island to Manhattan Supreme Court escorted by two police cars. As we pulled up to the court building, I heard a crowd chanting, "Free the Panther 21. All power to the people." I peeked through the grated window slit and saw a hundred or so Panthers standing in military formation in front of the building. Directly behind them were several hundred demonstrators—white, Latino, black—a rainbow of people pumping their fists and shouting. I knew that twenty-one of us had been indicted (although three or four eluded arrest on the morning of April 2), so this demonstration was for us. We were the Panther 21. I shouted "Power to the people!" through the vent in the window as the hell wagon sped by the demonstrators.

The cops turned me over to court officers who led me to a courtroom. I saw Afeni, Lumumba, Dhoruba, and the rest of the incarcerated Panther 21. We greeted each other with clenched fists. We were flanked by William Kunstler, Gerald Lefcourt, and several other lawyers who had become part of our defense team. The court clerk read off the counts of the superseding indictment. More conspiracy charges and overt acts had been added. The lawyers asked that our bail be lowered. They related stories of neglect, abuse, and torture that had been inflicted on members of the Panther 21. Many were being held in dirty isolation cells and denied visitors. Several had been attacked by guards. Lee Berry, twenty-four, a Vietnam vet who developed epilepsy from wounds received in combat, had experienced a series of seizures and had been denied medical treatment.

The judge denied all motion for bail reduction as well as any change in prison treatment. At this point Lumumba called the judge a fascist and asked, "Why don't you just sentence us right now and get it over with since we're being railroaded." Dhoruba and other Panthers shouted out Panther slogans and insults.

The Panthers were unmatched in ability when it came to verbal assaults and kung fu dialogue. Signifying, sounding down, or playing the dozens was an oral and cultural tradition in the black community. Verbal sparring could break out at a party, on a street corner, or in the subway. The person who delivered the sharpest, funniest, and most degrading lines about their opponent's looks, relations, or status won. "I'll slap the taste out your mouth, you tree-jumping, welfare cheese-eating, nobody-wants-your-greasy-ass jackrabbit son of a bitch." The Panthers combined the blunt-force gut shot of a dozens-style insult with a razor slash of revolutionary politics.

So when presiding Judge John Murtagh, a white-haired conservative racist who liked to present himself as refined and scholarly, was called "a foul-breathed, lynching, grand-dragon-looking, fascist pig," he was stunned. Defendants weren't supposed to speak in court, especially not his court. They were supposed to communicate through their lawyers, especially if they were poor black defendants who were facing hundreds of years in prison. They were usually docile because they were genuinely afraid or because they were playing the role of "repentant" before the all-powerful white courts. But Murtagh now had a courtroom full of "uppity niggers" who felt nothing but contempt and rage for a system that denied them their rights and treated them like animals.

Our radical attorneys were not much better. When Judge Murtagh would instruct them to quiet us down, they would press the case for lower bail and humane treatment, emphasizing that we (the Panthers) had a right to be outraged at our treatment. Over a chorus of "Power to the people," "Death to the pigs," "Get your motherfuckin' hands off me," Murtagh banged his gavel and we were escorted from the courtroom.

The lawyers were able to convince Murtagh to allow us an attorney-client conference in the holding cell. Tempers were still running high when the guards opened the cell door and let in the attorneys, along with Afeni Shakur and Joan Bird from the women's cell. It was now clear that this wasn't just a trumped-up "meatball" of a case that was going to be dismissed. They had arrested the entire leadership of the New York Black Panther Party and were trying to put us away for the rest of our lives. I learned how the cops had pointed guns at children and hit Panthers with gun butts during the April 2 raids. The content of apartments and homes had been trashed and destroyed during the searches. Wives and children were struggling for food and shelter while their mates and fathers were in jail.

Members of the Panther 21 provided for their families with jobs ranging from community organizer (Afeni Shakur) and transit authority worker (Kwando Kinshasha) to computer engineer (Sundiata Acoli) and biochemical researcher (Dr. Curtis Powell). In our ranks were a visual artist (Dhoruba Bin Wahad), a poet (Kwesi Balagoon), a writer (Cetewayo Tabor), a film lab technician (Shaba Om), a laborer (Baba Odinga), and a military veteran (Ali Bey Hassan).

The Panthers formed a fearsome military column when they lined up in black berets and leather coats. Beneath the berets were young men and women who had come to realize that their individual problems were connected to all oppressed people. Students, veterans, ex-convicts, young mothers, workers, street people—the composition of the Panther 21 reflected the broad membership of the Black Panther Party. They were the folks that Malcolm X called "the grassroots" and that

Frantz Fanon called "the wretched of the earth," coming together to study, work, and sacrifice in a movement that articulated their frustration, their rage, and their need for positive action to change the conditions around them.

"What the hell is going on with these trumped-up charges?" the Panthers wondered out loud as we huddled around our attorneys. The lawyers still didn't have a clear picture of District Attorney Hogan's case against us. They had been frustrated at every turn at their attempts to get information even with the court rules of pretrial discovery. But one thing they had learned was that the New York chapter had been infiltrated.

"There are two undercover cops who say they were there for all of the meetings and all of the training," Gerald Lefcourt said. "They are part of a special undercover unit known as BOSS—Bureau of Special Services. One of the cops' name is Gene Roberts." I knew who Gene was. Brother Gene, as we called him, had been a Black Muslim and Malcolm X's bodyguard. He was three feet away from Malcolm when he was shot at the Audubon Ballroom in Harlem. There was a photo in *Life* magazine of Gene Roberts giving Malcolm mouth-to-mouth resuscitation as Malcolm's body lay on the stage covered in blood.

"Brother Gene is a pig? I can't believe it," one of the Panthers said.

"The other cop is Ralph White."

"Who the hell is Ralph White?" someone asked.

Gerry read another name from the court papers. "The name he used in the Panthers was Yedwa."

Time stopped when I heard Yedwa's name. Head spinning, heart pounding, brain contracting. Yedwa was a cop? He was my teacher, my mentor, my big brother. The father I never had. He came to my house and convinced Noonie to let me come back to the Panther office. How the hell could this be?

Afeni broke the silence that had numbed the room. "I'm not surprised," she said. "Yedwa always acted like a reckless agent provocateur. I knew he was a pig." Afeni was a fiery Panther leader who never held back her opinions or edited her feelings. She and Yedwa had often argued about his brazen comments and reckless behavior. We had considered Yedwa a "crazy nigga"; Afeni considered him dangerous, and in the open forum of a stormy Panther meeting had called him a pig. Lumumba censured Afeni, saying that she was being "over-emotional" and that such accusations should not be made between comrades without concrete proof.

But now the truth was undeniably and disgustingly upon us. Yedwa was a pig. I wrapped myself in anger. The feeling of betrayal was too hard to process. I mumbled something like, "Yedwa is a traitorous pig," as the guards came to take us back to our various jails. Like a zombie, I allowed myself to be handcuffed and loaded into the paddy wagon. By the time I was processed back into Rikers it was 1 a.m. I fell into a deep, coma-like sleep.

8

When Prison Doors Open, Dragons Fly Out

I was still numb when the guards woke us up the next morning by turning on the cell lights and blaring the "Get ready to lockout for breakfast" announcement on the loudspeakers. I had a dream about the Panthers ambushing the armored hell wagon on the highway and breaking me out, the assault team led by Yedwa, who explained that he was a double agent who infiltrated the police force on behalf of the revolution. The clanging of cell doors opening brought me back to reality. "Yedwa is a pig!" I declared to myself. If you see him, then it's

SOS, which was Panther terminology for "shoot on sight." I stepped out of my cell a different person. I felt detached from my surroundings. Like I was in prison, but not. Like I was alive, but not.

Yedwa, Kinshasha, and other Panthers who were combat veterans talked about the "I don't give a fuck whether I live or die" attitude necessary for survival on the battlefield. Soldiers who cared about living and making it back home alive were usually the ones who got wasted. My cell partner, Manny, talked about the "don't give a fuck" attitude as it related to doing time. "Dudes that walk around worried about what their girl is doing on the outside and whether or not they're going to make their parole date always draw bad luck," Manny said. "They usually get jacked up by somebody because they're thinking about the street instead of concentrating on doing time." I walked down the tier as cool as can be. Anyone checking my face would have seen a vacant, combat look in my eyes. I had been arrested, beaten, betrayed and was probably going to get a life sentence. What more could they do, other than kill me? The last twenty-four hours had bitch-slapped the self-pity and fear out of me. I was a young soldier now. This was war. My mission was to make revolution, and I no longer gave a fuck.

Ho Chi Minh, the leader of North Vietnam, wrote, "When prison doors open dragons fly out." I adopted this as a personal mantra along with Malcolm X's quote, "The Penitentiary has been the University for many a black man." Adolescent boys usually left prison as jail-hardened men who learned to be better thieves, robbers, and drug dealers from their fellow prisoners. I was determined to be a better revolutionary and to create an army of dragons who would be ready to fly out when the prison doors opened or were broken down. I managed to smuggle back some Black Panther newspapers and several books in the stack of legal documents the lawyers had given each of us in court. The guards that strip-searched you when you returned from a court trip were more interested in finding drugs, money, or filter cigarettes than written materials, and I was able to sneak in more books and literature with each court trip. Soon I had a small library ranging from Frederick Douglass to Che Guevara. I organized study groups and political education classes. We tutored the guys who couldn't read and started martial arts classes. All this happened after I did thirty days in the hole for attacking Lefty.

I walked into the day room the day after I learned about Yedwa. The day room was a large recreation room that contained a Ping-Pong table, card tables, and chairs set up in front of a mounted television. I stood near the back of the rec room watching the evening news. Lefty was at a card table playing blackjack for cigarettes.

"What's up, baby?" he said, squeezing his crotch as he smiled at me.

"My name is Jamal. All right?" I answered in an annoyed voice.

Lefty and the other inmates at the card table chuckled and went back to their game. I watched the news for a few more minutes and left.

Lunch the next day was mashed potatoes, gravy, and ground meat patties, or "murder burgers," named that because they were so hard to digest. I came off the mess-hall line carrying my tray and passed Lefty who was sitting at a table with the rest of the house gang.

"What's going on, baby?" Lefty called out as I passed.

I froze, stomach curling into a tight knot. "I told you my name is Jamal."

"Yeah, all right, baby," Lefty said with a sneer, "or maybe I'll call you Panther baby." He laughed and took a bite of his murder burger.

Before I even realized what was happening, I smashed Lefty in the face with my tray. Lefty fell back, his legs still hooked around the seating bench. "Oh shit," he cried as he tried to swing up at me. I clubbed him three more times, then began to stomp and kick him as he writhed on the ground.

"I ain't nobody's baby. You hear me, motherfucker? I'm a man!"

Lefty was stunned. Blood from his nose and mouth mixed with the mashed potatoes and ground meat I had smashed into his face. I tried to turn the table over on him as Merciful struggled to hold me back. "That's enough, man, you got him," he said, trying to calm me down. "You gonna catch another case."

I punched and shoved Merciful and tried to get back at Lefty who had pulled himself to one knee. Guards were now on the scene. Several grabbed me and handcuffed me and carried me out of the mess hall. Captain Woods and the disciplinary committee gave me thirty days in the bing for fighting. "You broke that boy's nose. You know that?" Captain Woods informed me. I just stared straight ahead. "I don't know who started it," Captain Woods said, "but I'm sure that guy had it coming."

I worked out three times a day in the bing. Jumping jacks, push-ups, sit-ups, and punching my rolled-up mattress like a heavy bag. I knew I would have to fight Lefty again and probably some of the house gang. I wondered if Manny would still lend me one of his figas. This situation had surely become life and death. Twenty-nine days later the guards took me back to Three Block.

Everyone was locked in their cell for the afternoon count when I walked down the tier. Every afternoon and evening inmates were locked in their cell and had to stand when the guards came by to count everyone. This was to make sure you were really in your cell and were still alive. As I passed the cells, various prisoners nodded and spoke: "Hey man, what's happening, Brother Jamal?" The guards locked me in the cell with Manny who told me that Lefty had been transferred upstate to serve his time. I still expected beef with the rest of the house gang, but they treated me with total respect. Merciful, whom I had punched, approached me in the day room. "We cool?" he asked.

"I'm cool if you're cool," I replied.

Merciful nodded and let me know that I now had a "rep" throughout the cell block and that I could have a spot on the house gang if I wanted.

"No thanks," I replied. "You know how I feel about that neocolonialist, slave overseer, Uncle Tom bullshit."

Merciful smiled. "You a heavy dude, you know that? A real black-power soldier." With that we banged fists and made peace.

MORE INMATES JOINED the PE classes and martial arts workout. We formed a prison cadre, complete with a code of conduct:.

> No juggling
> No booty bandits
> No hard drugs
> No collaborating with the guards

We formed a cooperative with our own stash of commissary items and toiletries. If a brother needed cigarettes or cookies, he borrowed it from the cooperative and paid it back on commissary day. If a new inmate came into the cell block, the cooperative would give him a little welcome pack with toiletries and a few basics to get him by until his first commissary day. The house gang and the jugglers didn't like what we were doing, but our cadre was about forty prisoners strong and we knew how to rumble.

The guards would often break up our meetings and workouts, calling it unlawful assembly, but we would simply reconfigure into smaller groups and continue our sessions. Captain Woods and other officials would stop by my cell to ask if everything was all right. I would smile and say, "Considering that I am a political prisoner of war in a concentration camp, everything is just swell."

The smuggled Panther literature and regular newspapers that reached me gave me a harsh sense of the battle being waged on the Black Panther Party by the government. FBI director J. Edgar Hoover testified before Congress in June 1969, saying, "The Black Panther Party without question is the greatest threat to the internal security of the country." Hoover used this moment to get Congress's blessing to wage a public as well as secret war against the Black Panther Party.

Every week I would read or hear about a Panther office being raided, Panthers being arrested, or Panthers being killed. Fred Hampton and Mark Clark were murdered when the Chicago police raided a Panther apartment there. Fred was a gifted speaker who was organizing the gangs in Chicago.

The police shot him multiple times as he lay asleep and unarmed in his bed inches away from his pregnant wife. Fred was twenty-one. Panther offices were bombed and destroyed in Newark, Denver, and Des Moines. Three days after Fred's murder, the Los Angeles police attacked the local headquarters in that city. The Panthers resisted, led by Deputy Minister of Defense Geronimo Pratt, and a sixteen-hour shootout ensued. I would sit in my cell at night thinking about fellow Panthers, some just a year or two older than me, wounded and dying on the street. I felt angry and at the same time frustrated and ashamed that I wasn't on the battlefield with them.

The prison cadre movement spread to other cell blocks. Young prisoners would pass in the hallway and salute each other with "Power to the people." The number of fights and incidents of rape dropped dramatically. We were allowed to go to the yard once or twice a week. Inmates would usually make a beeline for the basketball court, shoving each other for the balls and team positions. One fall day we entered the yard and no one ran for a ball. The basketballs, footballs, and softballs just lay on the ground. Instead we lined up across the yard and started performing a karate kata that I had taught the inmates. Captain Woods and the other officials watched.

Around 2 a.m. the next morning Captain Woods and a team of guards came to my cell. "You're being transferred, Mr. Joseph," Captain Woods informed me.

"What are you putting me in the bing for?" I protested.

"It's not the bing. You're going to another prison."

The cell door rolled opened, and Manny jumped into a fighting stance. There were about twenty guards outside. We had "no wins" in this situation.

"It's cool, brother," I said, patting Manny on the shoulder. "I'll be all right." I gathered a few things, leaving most of my books and commissary with Manny.

"Watch your back, bro," Manny said with clenched fists. "Walk slow and drink plenty of cold water."

A police escort drove me to the Queens House of Detention, commonly known as Branch Queens. I was processed and taken to the segregation floor. All my Panther comrades were there. Our lawyers had finally secured a court order directing the Department of Corrections to house us together so we could prepare for trial. Corrections had previously resisted these requests, saying that we were high security risks. We had all been organizing in our various prisons. The authorities now realized it was a greater risk to their security to have Panthers on the loose in the general prison population. So with the exception of Joan Bird and Afeni Shakur, who were still in the Women's House of Detention, we were now all in one unit.

Our cells filled with documents and law books as we prepared for trial. Eight months had gone by and our lawyers were still fighting to see all of the evidence that would be presented at our trial. We would fill the tiny conference room and talk about how to fight the case. William Kunstler had left the defense team to begin the Chicago Eight trial. Bobby Seale, Abbie Hoffman, Tom Hayden, and other radical leaders were accused of conspiracy charges growing out of demonstrations that happened at the 1968 Democratic Convention in Chicago. Bobby, the cofounder and chairman of the Black Panther Party, had been bound, shackled, and gagged in the courtroom when he demanded to defend himself. Like Dred Scott, a man who was remanded by the courts back to slavery a hundred years earlier, Bobby's treatment reflected the legal opinion written by the Supreme Court in Scott's case, which said, "A black man has no rights that a white man is bound to respect." We knew we were being railroaded and that we had to make our trial a symbol of resistance.

Gerry Lefcourt had become our lead attorney. He was twenty-six years old and had only tried one major case before this. I knew he was nervous about being lead counsel when so many lives were at stake.

"You can do it, brother," Lumumba said to Gerry. "Besides they're giving us three hundred years no matter what goes down, so just give 'em hell."

There were other young attorneys who had come to join the fight too: Carol Lefcourt (Gerry's sister-in-law); Bob Bloom; Sandy Katz; Marty Stolar; Bill Crain (who was my attorney); and Charles McKinney, a distinguished older African American attorney who had enormous trial experience.

Afeni announced that she had decided to defend herself. She had read Fidel Castro's book *History Will Absolve Me.* Fidel, himself a young attorney, had been facing life in prison for acts of insurrection against Batista's Cuban government. He told the court that no matter what sentence it imposed, history would prove that the idea of revolution was just and timely. Afeni wanted to address the court and the jury to let them know that she was a "freedom fighter." Lumumba and other Panthers protested, saying that Afeni would get too emotional. Afeni stood firm, declaring that since nobody else was going to do her three hundred years, nobody else could tell her how to defend herself. I agreed with Afeni, although it was clear that her decision was not up for vote. Cetewayo "Cet" Tabor announced that he would defend himself as well. There was less resistance to his decision. Cet was an eloquent speaker with a booming, Paul Robeson basso profundo voice. Charles McKinney and the other attorneys agreed that it would be good to have Panthers address the jury directly.

At night I lay in my cell thinking about a three-hundred-year sentence. I would escape, I thought, or the revolution would succeed and the walls of Jericho would come tumbling down. But if I had to do life and die in prison, I could handle it. I had done a week when I didn't think I could last a day. I did a month when a week seemed impossible. Now it was almost a year and I could do the time "standing on my head," like the older prisoners said. My only regret was that I had never done more than French kiss a girl as we slow danced at a party. I was sixteen years old, facing 368 years in prison, and still a virgin.

There were a few more trips to court as we fought to have our bail lowered and to win pretrial motions to have the charges dismissed. Judge Murtagh would always rule against us. We would invariably turn the proceedings upside down with statements and outbursts that let the judge know how we felt about the "racist, fascist legal lying" he was trying to put down.

Back in our special prison unit the older Panthers tutored me in political and military theory. I studied Suntzu's *The Art of War*, Hannibal's military campaigns, and the battle strategies that had been used by freedom fighters in Africa and Latin America. We had in-depth discussions about Marx, Mao, and Che and went deep into the writings and speeches of African revolutionaries like Patrice Lumumba, Sekou Torre, and Amílcar Cabral. Dhoruba, Cetewayo, and Lumumba were professor-like in their teaching and demands. I had to write essays and critically defend my positions. If prison was a university, as Malcolm said, then our Panther wing was grad school.

I had stopped counting the days that I was in prison. Like most men and women who are locked up for a long period, a prisoner learns to start counting months. Counting days makes you crazy. You think about the home-cooked meal you're missing or who your lover is messing with on the outside. You trip about the hundreds of days left in your bid and wonder if you can keep it together. Your mind slips into thoughts and ways to beat the bed and eventually into thoughts of suicide. Better to count the months. Ask any prisoner how long they've been in, and he will tell you the time in months. Prisoners doing really long sentences will start counting the years. "Been down eighteen years, youngblood," one lifer told me, "and I'm never gonna see daylight."

I had been down eleven months when the guards came to take me to court. They didn't want my codefendants, just me, saying I had a special hearing. The older Panthers stood around me and demanded that the guard show us the court appearance order. The appearance was listed as a hearing to review a motion about my youthful offender status. I forgot that my lawyer filed this motion months ago and was surprised it hadn't been dismissed along with all the other motions. The Panther wall parted, and Lumumba told me to go to court.

The hearing was in a small courtroom. No supporters. No army of court guards. I stood next to my attorney, Bill Crain, who argued to Judge Murtagh that this was my first offense and that I was an honor student who was involved in church and community organizations. The hefty, perpetually annoyed assistant district attorney Joseph Phillips agreed that I was intelligent but argued that I had allowed myself to be influenced by violent revolutionaries and had turned my intelligence to illegal subversive activities. I took a deep breath to gather enough oxygen for a long stream of insults at Phillips. Bill Crain nudged me and whispered, "Just be cool." Judge Murtagh then asked Mr. Phillips if he objected to the youthful offender motion. "The People have no objection, Your Honor." It always pissed us off when the prosecution referred to themselves and their case as "the People," as in *The People of the State of New York vs. Lumumba Shakur and the Black Panther Party*.

I was so involved in my negative reflexive gut reaction to Phillips's use of the word "people" that it didn't register that he wasn't objecting. "The motion is granted and the defendant Eddie Joseph, also known as Jamal Joseph, is hereby adjudicated a youthful offender. Since he can no longer be tried as an adult, he is severed from the case."

What? I thought, now trying to process the hearing.

"In view of Mr. Joseph's YO status we request that he be released on his own recognizance," Bill Crain said.

"Some bail should be imposed, Judge," Phillips countered. "Even with YO status there is still a possibility of a four-year prison sentence."

"Bail is set at ten thousand dollars," Murtagh declared. He adjourned the hearing. Phillips and Judge Murtagh left the courtroom. Bill Crain smiled, congratulated me, and told me that I would probably be out on bail in a day or two.

I was totally troubled when I returned to the Panther wing. I didn't want to leave my comrades behind and I definitely didn't want to be thought of as a "youthful offender." I had done eleven months in jail like a man. Now a judge had gone and made me a boy? The older Panthers told me to stop trippin'. Panthers were needed on the street fighting, not rotting in jail.

"If the gods forgot to lock your cell and you had a chance to escape, would you split and come back for us? Or would you stay behind like a knucklehead?" Dhoruba asked.

"The answer is obvious to a duck," I replied sarcastically, "but this is different."

"No different," I was told in a collective voice. "We need you out there raising awareness and bail money with Sister Afeni."

Afeni had been released two weeks earlier when the Panther 21 Defense Committee had raised enough money to post her hundred-thousand-dollar bail. We took a vote among ourselves and chose Afeni as the best person to represent the 21 on the outside. We felt a broader section of people could relate to her as a black woman who was being framed. Now that my bail had been lowered, it was my turn to spread our message. People would also respond to me as a young student who had been kidnapped by the pigs from his grandmother's home.

The next night the deputy warden and two guards told me

I was being released on bail. I had been in prison for eleven months, from April 1969 to February 1970. So much had happened inside that it felt more like three years. I was embraced by my comrades and then led from the unit. I signed a discharge paper and stepped through the barred gate into a cold February night. Afeni was waiting for me along with two Panther officers from California who had been sent to work in New York after our arrest. Afeni gave me a crushing hug. The brothers gave me a Panther handshake and welcomed me home. A car was waiting. Before I got in I looked up at the barred windows on the ninth floor. That was the location of the Panther wing. Dhoruba had made me promise to yell something back at the jail when I got out. As promised, I cupped my hands and shouted, "You pigs kiss my mother-fuckin' ass!" Dhoruba and the other Panthers yelled back at me, "Power to the people!" The California Panthers shook their heads and laughed. "You New York niggas sure is crazy." We climbed into a black sedan and sped off toward Harlem.

9

Blood and Wine

The streets of Harlem looked good as we cruised through the night. Even the run-down tenements and junkies wandering the street were welcome sights. I was out of the concentration camp and back in the black colony. It was a weeknight, but the bars along Seventh Avenue, the Gold Lounge and the Shalimar, were jumping like it was a Saturday night—street folks and hustlers hanging out front, flashy cars pulling up.

We drove across the bridge to the South Bronx where a new Panther office had opened. It was called the East Coast

Ministry of Information and had been designated as the official headquarters for East Coast Panther operations. It was a large storefront office, three times as big as the Harlem office. The office was packed with new faces. Many had joined the party in the last year; others were Panthers from other cities who had been transferred to New York to help keep the chapter there running after the arrest of the Panther 21. I was engulfed with a chorus of "Power to the people," "Welcome home, brother," and Panther handshakes and hugs as I moved through the room. I felt awkward and dizzy. The scene was overwhelming. Everyone knew my name and was giving me a hero's welcome. But I knew I was just a nervous man-child getting out of jail.

Anyone fresh out the joint will tell you that readjustment is a bitch. You feel like everyone can see your prison number tattooed on your forehead. Handling money, ordering food, buying knickknacks in a store, and getting on subways where people are pushing and shoving is a cold shock. You've just been released from a world where there is imposed structure, lines, order, solitude, and no menu choices. It may be steel and concrete, but it's familiar and home bitter home. I'd only been in prison for eleven months, but it was enough to be contaminated with the virus of institutionalization. And on my first night out even the friendly crush of adoring Panthers was an overload.

I was grateful that Afeni was right there introducing me to

people and pulling me to the side when she saw me getting stressed. "You all right?" she asked.

"Real cool," came my automatic, show-no-weakness response. What was I supposed to say? That I was really shittin' bricks and that I wished I was back in Branch Queens jail with the rest of the 21?

"Call your grandmother," Afeni said firmly. "Let her know you're out and you're okay."

I spun the rotary dial. Noonie answered after the second ring. "It's me, Noonie. I'm out," I said cheerfully, trying to hide the Panther voices and the James Brown music playing in the background.

"Praise the Lord," she intoned. "Where are you?"

"At the Panther office," I replied meekly. Silence. I could tell she wasn't happy I didn't come straight home and that I made my first stop the Panthers.

"When will you be home?" she asked, as if I were calling in late from a basketball game or a community center dance. Hell, I just got out of prison.

"Soon," I said respectfully.

I knew Noonie would be watching from the front window so I declined a lift in the Panther car and took the subway with money that Afeni pressed into my hand. I hugged Noonie a long time when I walked in the door. She seemed smaller and older than before. We sat and talked a long time. There wasn't much I felt I could share about my prison experiences. Instead

I listened to church and neighborhood stories as I relished the home-cooked meal she prepared for me.

The next day Noonie and I walked to Evander Childs High School to reenroll me. The guidance counselor told me he was placing me in the tenth grade. "But I was in the eleventh grade," I protested. "Two more months and I would have been promoted to the twelfth." The guidance counselor made some calls and said there was nothing he could do. The principal and the superintendent's office all said that I had to repeat tenth grade. These people were trippin'! I had been an honor student with no marks lower than 85. I had skipped eighth grade as a Special Progress student, and was well on my way to graduate high school at sixteen and a half. No way was I down with this charade.

"The fascist board of miseducation is collaborating with the government swine to deny me my rights," I shouted as I jumped to my feet.

Noonie would have broken my shin with a kick had I been close enough, but instead I caught a stiff "Eddie, sit down and be respectful." Even though she was embarrassed by my outburst, she saw my point. "I don't know why they're making you repeat a grade," Noonie said as we walked home through the chilly February air. "You should be getting ready for graduation now." All I could do was shrug. I was sure that the cops and FBI had been around to the school to make sure that I was given a hard time.

There were a number of alternative schools called street academies that opened as a result of community activists' struggle for more meaningful community-based education. These certified schools were having success educating kids who had dropped out or were having a difficult time in regular schools. Noonie agreed to let me check out one of the street academies.

I enrolled in a school called Harlem Prep, short for Harlem Preparatory Academy. It was a large storefront located near 135th Street and Eighth Avenue. The curriculum featured math and science classes along with black and African history courses that weren't part of the regular school curriculum. The director and most of the teachers were black and prided themselves on their ability to engage students and to get them into college. They knew I was a Black Panther out on bail and welcomed me. Class discussions were open and Afrocentric. When I spoke, I felt like I was joining in a real forum of ideas instead of battling a teacher who was trying to brainwash the students. After class I would walk downtown to the Panther office where I would help sell newspapers, run meetings, or be out in the community organizing.

At night Panthers would meet back at the office or at one of the "Panther pads" (an apartment or a house that had been set up as a Panther commune) for a meal, some wine, music, and a few short hours in bed—sometimes alone but most of the times with another exhausted Panther or with a Panther lover. A bed was often nothing more than a mattress on the floor, sometimes two or three mattresses in the room.

Three days after I got out of jail I spent the night at a Panther pad. I had been all over the city selling Panther newspapers with an eighteen-year-old Panther girl named Sheila. We started out with a group of other Panthers along 125th Street, then left the "black colony" to head downtown to Times Square and then the Village, so we could sell the remainder of our papers in "the mother country." We'd duck in and out of bars listening to rock music on Bleecker Street, and we hung out in Washington Square Park watching hippies dance around the fountain. By the time we got to the Panther pad on 153rd Street all the food was gone, so we whipped up some leftovers and ate in the kitchen. Sheila and I brushed against each other as we were doing dishes. A bolt of electricity shot from my loins to my brain. Of course, I didn't know what to do except say "Excuse me" and soap up another dish. It was close to midnight when I grabbed my coat to head back to the Bronx.

"I know you ain't trying to get out on the street this time of night, brother," said Jacob, a Panther who was wearing sweatpants as pajamas. "The pigs out there are like vampires, just waiting to vamp on a Panther rollin' by himself."

That was all the prodding I needed. I picked up the wall phone and dialed Noonie. I told her I was staying at a friend's house and would be home in the morning. She wasn't pleased, but at least I had called.

I undressed down to my T-shirt and socks, keeping my pants on, and lay on the narrow couch. Sheila said I could crash on her mattress. When I told her I was fine on the couch, she took me by the hand and led me to her room, which looked like it had been a large closet. It had no window and was barely able to accommodate a full-size mattress. I lay next to Sheila like a train rail, scared to move. The apartment was quiet. Most of the other Panthers were knocked out. "You always sleep with your pants on?" Sheila teased. She had a pretty smile and wore only a baggy T-shirt and panties. I jettisoned my pants and tossed them in the corner. Sheila lay with her back to me. She nudged closer and guided my arm around her waist. I got up my courage and kissed her on the neck. She moved even closer and turned to me. We kissed. We helped each other out of our remaining clothes and got under the covers. Sheila could tell I was a virgin. She slowed me down and taught me how to move. We made love until we fell asleep in each other's arms.

I walked into Noonie's apartment around eleven o'clock the next morning. Noonie was angry, but she didn't yell or scold. Instead she sat on the couch sewing and told me that I could not use her house like a motel. I needed to be in by a certain time and that was that. I took a deep breath and told Noonie what I had been thinking about on the long subway ride home. "I'm leaving, Ma. There's too much work to do for the revolution and I need to be with the party." My words hit

Noonie like a heavy weight, and she sagged. She wanted to continue life where we left off. Church, Sunday dinner, school conferences, watching a show on the black-and-white TV together on the worn but comfortable couch. I wanted to spend all my time agitating, fighting, and hanging with my Panther comrades. Plus I had slept with a woman. No way was I letting Noonie tuck me in at 10 p.m. in her house when sexy Panther women like Sheila were willing to share their beds with me.

I reminded Noonie that both she and Pa B. had left home when they were teenagers.

"But times were different," Noonie said with worry.

"Times are worse," I responded, "and I need to be out there in the struggle."

I expected Noonie to call our pastor or another family friend to talk sense to me, but she didn't. I spent one more night at the apartment, then next morning packed a few things. Noonie gave me a long hug and fifty dollars to see me on my way. I could feel her heart beating as she held me close. Part of me wanted to turn back and be the man-child again—safe and spoiled by Grandma. But scar tissue had already grown over my youth. I let Noonie go and headed out the door to battle—without looking back.

There was one more family visit I needed to make. Noonie told me that my maternal grandmother, Alita, had been calling her the whole time I was in prison. Since Alita spoke no English, my little sister, Elba, would do the telephone

Spanish–English translations. Elba was now thirteen and Luis was eleven. I thought my family might be reluctant, perhaps even ashamed, to see me, but my brother and sister opened the front door of their Brownsville house and jumped into my arms. Alita cried tears of joy. We sat at the kitchen table eating a home-cooked Cuban feast. My Spanish was poor at best, but I clearly understood the love and the prayers as Alita squeezed my hand and told me to be safe. That night I stayed at a Panther pad in Brooklyn and headed back to Harlem the next day.

The life of the full-time Panther wasn't as romantic as I thought it would be. Life in the Panther pad was tough. The Panthers, especially those in the Harlem branch, were poor as shit. The boiler in our tenement building was old and out of commission two or three times a week. Even though we had organized a rent strike and were making repairs ourselves, the building was in sad shape. It was February, and the rags and blankets stuffed in the cracked windows did not keep the cold out. Lovemaking could keep you warm for a while, but Sheila and I would have to put on sweat clothes and sometimes coats on those frigid nights.

Picture dragging yourself from exhausted sleep, out of whatever little warmth you had in your bed, to boil water to wash up and head out into the cold to start work at a Panther breakfast program, where all Panthers were required to work. Getting up at five and trudging through the freezing cold with three hours of sleep took commitment, although once you made it to the church or community center basement you were energized by the kids. They were glad to be there and happy to have a hot meal provided by the Panthers. We would have them sing songs, and we'd talk about black history and love for the community as we served pancakes, eggs, cereal, and juice.

By eight o'clock, the kids were gone and the pots and pans were scrubbed and put away. From there I walked ten blocks to my classes at Harlem Prep. I was freezing. My only winter clothing was a thin leather jacket and a light sweater.

One afternoon I stood shivering on a corner of 125th Street selling Panther papers. A community activist named Sayeed, one of the Harlem Five, took me to his apartment in the Lincoln projects and gave me a long army-style coat out of his closet, and Afeni made the Panther finance officer give me twenty dollars so I could buy a pair of warm shoes. Now I was really ready for the cold—bring on the revolution!

My classes at Harlem Prep ran from 9 a.m. till noon. Afternoons were spent selling newspapers and community organizing. The Panther paper was the main source of income for the party. Panthers got to keep five cents from each twenty-five-cent paper. The rest went to the chapter and national headquarters. So selling a hundred papers meant five dollars. And five dollars meant carfare, a meal, and a dollar or two in your pocket. There were no salaries, so if your stomach was growling at lunchtime or you needed to take a train or a bus someplace, then you'd better sell some papers.

There was usually a collective pot of food for dinner at the office or Panther pad. Our best cook was a three-hundred-pound, six-foot-five-inch intimidating-looking Panther named Bashir. Bashir could cook a pot of stew or fry a pile of chicken that would bring tears to your eyes. He was truly a gentle giant. When a group of racist white militia men jumped out of their cars and stood in military formation outside the Panther office, Bashir whipped most of their asses as a small crowd of Harlem residents cheered. I got in a few punches, but it was Bashir that put them on the run. A few minutes later he was laughing and crawling around on the floor of the Panther office as five kids rode on his back.

Bashir and I would go out together to seek donations for the Panther breakfast program. His size would give my smile the advantage we needed as we asked local merchants to donate milk, eggs, and cereal to the program. We were careful not to make threats or ask for money. A few storekeepers had been shaken down by fake Panthers in uniform demanding cash to protect their stores. A couple of these fakers were caught and given a real Panther ass-whipping. Bashir and I would invite the store owners to see the breakfast program in action before they gave. We wanted them to be assured that their donations were going straight to the community. Most of the store owners would donate once they saw the program. Some would give us additional canned goods, rice, and vegetables that made it possible to have food giveaway programs.

A lot of white high school and college kids would come to the Panther office to buy papers, books, and buttons and to attend the Wednesday night community PE classes. I became friends with a high school kid named Neal from New Jersey. On Saturdays he would bring his Volkswagen van and help us pick up boxes of food donated by merchants in the community for the breakfast program. An older Jewish man, who ran a nearby dry cleaner, also became a supporter. He would give us unclaimed clothes and would clean donated clothes for free, which we would set out on racks for the community. Dozens of people got free bags of food and free clothing from the Panther office each week.

Teenage activists from around the city came to the Harlem office to train and work as Panthers. Among them was Nile Rodgers, who later started the band Chic and became a famed musician, composer, and producer of hundreds of songs, including "We Are Family"; Joseph Harris, who became a physician and part of the Nobel Prize–honored "Doctors without Borders"; and Charles Barron, who is now a New York City councilman.

With so many of the Panther men being arrested and killed, women took on key leadership roles in the Panthers, running many of the programs and offices around country. Sisters Wonda, Safiyah, and Claudia kept the Harlem office going against all odds. Malika held the fort in Brooklyn, and Sister Audrey led the fight in Boston.

A Panther sister named Olewa, who was a trained nurse, organized a free storefront health clinic in Brooklyn, which was open on Saturdays and several afternoons a week to give free care to community folks who might otherwise not have been able to see a doctor. It was also the place where Panthers from Harlem, the Bronx, and Queens could go for health care.

It's amazing how sick we all were. A number of young Panthers, including me, had ulcers, directly related to stress and poor diets. Many of the young women suffered gynecological problems, also related to stress. High blood pressure and migraines were common. We would drink the chalky antacids, dry swallow the aspirins, and say, "Fuck it, we'll be dead in battle soon anyway."

I did a lot of speaking engagements on behalf of the Panther 21, both alone and with Afeni. I was giving at least one speech a day, sometimes more—at schools, community centers, and churches; on college campuses; even at the Apollo Theater. The biggest trip was speaking at cocktail-party fundraisers in the homes of the rich and the elite. The Panther 21 Defense Committee was organized soon after our arrest, and many members were young white activists. The Panthers and the committee separated the issues of civil liberties from the belief in Panther ideology and created a way for people from diverse backgrounds to join the conversation.

Composer Leonard Bernstein and other prominent Manhattanites opened their homes for cocktail fund-raisers, a "sixties happening" that author Tom Wolfe called "radical chic." The Panthers called it fund-raising and consciousness raising. From the days of the Underground Railroad and the abolitionist movement, white people of conscience have committed time, money, sweat, and sometimes blood to the cause of social justice.

Not long after the Panther 21 arrest, a group of young white radical students were taken into custody for planting a bomb at a government building. They were released on low bail. Members of the Minutemen, a white separatist group, were arrested with bombs and guns, and they were also released on low bail. The exorbitant bail levied in the Panther 21 case was a key organizing point used by our supporters. Why are there two standards—one black, one white—for justice in America? The next logical question raised at these events was whether the Panthers or any person of color could receive a fair trial.

I would often find myself in an elegant town house or penthouse talking about these issues and raising money for the Panther Bail Fund. An hour or two later I would be back in Harlem trying to grab three hours of sleep in a rat- and roach-infested tenement.

Another celebrity who supported us was the actress Jane Fonda. I first met her when she came by the Harlem office one afternoon to pick up some papers and pamphlets about political prisoners. Her hair was cut short and straight, and she wore no makeup and had on jeans, so I didn't recognize her. I guess I was expecting Barbarella, who had titillated my fourteen-year-old eyeballs a few months before I joined the Panthers. "Hi, I'm Jane," she said, extending her hand. She was relaxed and down-to-earth. She played with the children in the office and asked questions about the community programs and the Panther 21 case. There were no bodyguards or escorts, just a waiting taxi to take her back to the set of her current movie, *Klute*.

She invited me to stop by USA/Filmways, where the film was being shot, which I gladly did. I had no idea that Harlem was the home to a major film studio. USA/Filmways took up most of the block between Second and Third Avenues on 127th Street. *The Godfather, Taking of the Pelham 123, The Cotton Club,* and *New Jack City* were some of the movies shot there. It was my first time on a film set. Watching Jane Fonda and Donald Sutherland act in the midst of the mass of lights, cameras, equipment, and people was a mind blower. Jane would talk to me between takes and explain how the different camera angles and shots would be cut together to create a scene in the film. When I left the studio a couple of hours later it was still light outside, although the scene inside had been a night bedroom scene. Wow! I thought. Film is powerful! No wonder the Panther leadership encouraged young progressive filmmakers to interview and to document us.

Ossie Davis and Ruby Dee, the "first couple" of black theater, Broadway and Hollywood, came to the Panther office to show support and to film fund-raising appeals for the Panther 21. Harry Belafonte, Henry Fonda, Leonard Bernstein, and the great French playwright and philosopher Jean Genet were among other celebrities who visited the Harlem Panther office.

I learned to love jazz by sitting in the front row of clubs and concerts given in support of the Panther 21. Carmen McRae, Freddie Hubbard, Rahsaan Roland Kirk, and Max Roach turned me on with amazing vocals and intense playing. After the shows we would hang with the jazz greats and listen to their war stories about the racism and struggles they encountered traveling around the country. A couple of the musicians told me they kept guns in their music cases and considered themselves Panthers long before there was a Black Panther Party. White musicians also performed benefit concerts. The Grateful Dead did a few concerts on the West Coast. The Young Rascals rocked the Apollo Theater with "Groovin,'" "Good Lovin'," and other hits to help us raise money in New York.

We did a lot of small-group fund-raising events for Manhattan's "upper crust." These talks were designed to connect human faces to the Panther movement and to educate people about the Panther 21. The media had portrayed us as hate-filled terrorists; Afeni and I would talk about our community programs and the lives of our fellow Panther 21 members. There were other groups and organizations that also came forward in support of the civil liberties of the Panthers. The Committee of Returned Volunteers, founded by former Peace Corps volunteers, held fund raisers for the Panther Bail Fund. Reverend Moore opened his church in Harlem for fund-raising concerts and dinners. The NAACP Legal Defense Fund sent lawyers to help the Panther 21 fight in court for a reasonable bail. We worked together as a community.

The bigger events like the outdoor rallies, rock concerts, and student takeovers were designed to fire up the masses. "Brothers and sisters, we are gathered here today because the time for revolution has come and because the fascist pigs of the power structure have got to go," I yelled through a bull-horn microphone to a crowd of several thousand students at Columbia University. They had once again taken over the campus, protesting the war in Vietnam. The steps of Low Library, the stately domed building that governs the center of the campus, was the stage for the rally. The large bronze statue of Alma Mater that sits in front of Low Library had been blindfolded with the North Vietnamese flag.

Students held signs and banners: STOP THE WAR and POWER TO THE PEOPLE. "Brothers and sisters," I continued, "what the pigs fear most is what we have here today. Solidarity! Black, white, red, brown, and yellow standing together. Students and community folks standing together. Children of the bourgeois and children of the lumpen proletariat standing together demanding complete and total liberation. That's why the pig police and the swine National Guard have been brutally attacking college campuses. When the pigs murdered students at Jackson State University in Mississippi they made it clear that they will kill any nigger who stands up, and when the pigs fired on white students at Kent State University in Ohio they made it clear that anybody who stands up is a nigger." The crowd of students and activists cheered.

I looked around and saw the riot-geared police standing on the fringes of campus. "So, brothers and sisters, if Columbia University doesn't recognize that the war in Vietnam is a war of capitalist exploitation being waged against oppressed people of color, and if it doesn't recognize that the United States pig military is occupying Vietnam the way the New York City pig department occupies Harlem, then you must do more than take over this campus today. You need to burn this motherfucker down." The students went crazy. I pumped my fist and left the makeshift stage with the crowd shouting, "Power to the people!" and "Free the Panther 21!"

I would usually be escorted to these events by one or two young Panthers, Mark Holder and his younger brother Kim, partly for security and partly to help sell the Panther papers, buttons, and posters that we brought along to the events. These were good community organizers and dedicated "people's soldiers" who had the skills to do battle if and when it came to that.

There were many young Panthers, the rank and file, who literally worked day and night to keep the New York chapter going, who didn't get the headlines or the media soundbites but who gave blood, sweat, tears, and in some cases their lives to the movement.

The Panther party I came home to from prison was different from the organization I left. When I joined in 1968, being a Panther was a part-time proposition. You were expected to represent Panther ideology and organize wherever you went. The requirements for being a full-fledged Panther meant coming to a couple of political education classes a week and occasional branch meetings. The barrage of raids, shoot-outs, and arrests now made things different. Panthers were expected to make a full-time commitment. It was no longer an after-work or after-school thing.

Panthers around the country lived communally in houses or apartments. The days began before dawn and ended late at night. After serving children at one of the free breakfast program locations, selling papers, organizing, attending meetings, and patrolling the community, you would stumble into the Panther pad exhausted. It didn't matter how sleep-deprived a Panther was at the end of the day, you were still expected to take your turn sitting at the window of a Panther house or office, on lookout for the police. There was a real expectation that the cops would raid our homes or offices with guns blazing. Fred Hampton was murdered in his bed as he slept next to his pregnant wife. Seventeen-year-old Bobby Hutton was shot eleven times in the back after Oakland cops told him to run down an alley. In Des Moines, Iowa, Philadelphia, Newark, Denver, and L.A. cops shot up, bombed, and raided Panther offices. Thirty-six Panthers had been killed and hundreds were in prison.

Of course, we didn't think one or two teenagers with guns could hold off a police assault force by themselves. The job of the Panthers on sentry duty was to sound the alert so that the children could be taken to the safest area of the Panther pad, and then calls could be made to attorneys, the press, and community supporters. In cities where Panthers were able to sound the alert on police raids, the death toll and the brutality were held to a minimum. Cops were reluctant to kill Panthers when a crowd of community folk, lawyers, and reporters were watching.

Still the raids continued, and many more Panthers would die. Every day we received phone calls and letters that promised death to Panthers. We knew that the police were trying to intimidate us and to scare us, to make us quit, close the Panther offices, and go home. Instead, the threats and intimidation strengthened our resolve to fight, and to die if necessary. That, of course, was exactly the reaction that the FBI and the government wanted, as witnessed by FBI Director Hoover's counterintelligence program, COINTELPRO, through which operatives infiltrated the Panthers and planted false information and evidence designed to create anger, distrust, and paranoia. At the same time, the FBI went to local police departments with "evidence" that the Panthers were gearing up for an attack.

Both sides were hyped and paranoid because of the disinformation. We all wondered who in our midst could be a "pig," and we knew that the bullet that killed you could come from the front or the back. Veteran Panthers looked at newer Panthers with suspicion and at each other with doubt. Was Sister So-and-So leaving for a week because her mother was really sick? Did Brother So-and-So get his assault charges dropped because of lack of evidence or because he made a deal?

I took the floor at one of our monthly central staff meetings to talk about the sense of paranoia in the party. "When I joined the Panthers two years ago, Panthers were on the offensive with community patrols, programs, and rallies. When you turned on the news you would see Panthers storming the state capital at Sacramento, or Bobby, Eldridge, or David verbally kicking ass doing an interview. Now, whenever you turn on the TV, there's a story about a Panther who's been busted or been killed. I wouldn't join today if I saw all this shit coming down on the party. And anyone who joins knowing all this shit is coming down has got to be a fool or a pig and we don't need either one. So I propose that we do a moratorium on new members and tighten the ranks."

My remarks got a healthy dose of applause and "right ons." Nonetheless, the officers decided to keep the membership ranks open. I disagreed, but I was a loyal Panther and followed orders. That night I again took my turn at the window of the Harlem Panther apartment, watching the street with fatigued, bloodshot eyes, waiting for the enemy to come.

10

Revolution in Our Lifetime

It was spring in Harlem, and people were in bloom on the streets. Children playing and beautiful women doing African ballets just by walking down the block. Hustlers and gangsters, challenging the eyes with green and yellow silk suits and red and gold Cadillacs.

I walked down the street with Raymond Masai Hewitt, who was the Panther minister of education in California. He liked walking through the community whenever he visited a local chapter. I had become part of the Panthers' National

Speakers Bureau. The senior leadership had seen me rap at various local fund-raisers for the Panther 21 and decided to make me part of the national speaking team. Masai taught me to walk through the poorest part of town anywhere I was appearing so I could talk about the local problems and issues in my speech. Many colleges and universities border poor communities, and we would try to fire up university students about conditions of poverty and police brutality that existed near their classrooms and dormitories. So in the shadow of Columbia University and the sunrise of the Apollo, Masai and I hung out with Harlem community folk; "the grassroots," as Malcolm called them; "the lumpen proletariat," as the Panthers called them.

There were two men—"lumpen brothers"—fighting on 120th Street. A small crowd was watching. I ran through the crowd and jumped in the middle of the action. Gently, but firmly, I pushed a short dude and a muscle-bound cat apart, without thinking, doing it like I did it all the time. "Don't fight, brothers," I shouted. "That's what the oppressor wants us to do—kill each other." Those words and my Black Panther buttons were usually enough to cool the situation. If there were no fellow Panthers present to help me, someone from the crowd usually stepped forward to help me keep the combatants apart. This time no one moved.

Masai yelled, "Jamal, he's got a knife."

I turned to see that "Shorty" had pulled a hunting knife

and was starting to swing at "Muscles," the guy I was holding. Swoosh. The blade swept by my ear as Shorty tried to leap over me to get his thrust in.

Common sense should have made me jump out of the way and run. But what young Panther has common sense? Instead I walked toward Shorty and his ten-inch blade.

"You want to kill somebody, brother? Kill me. That's all the pigs want to see is another dead nigga. Any dead nigga will do."

"But I ain't got no beef with you," Shorty snarled. He sidestepped me so he could lunge at Muscles.

I pushed his knife aside and yelled at Muscles over my shoulder, "Split, man. Run!" Muscles blended into the crowd and made his retreat. "It's over, brother," I yelled at Shorty. "He's gone."

By this time Masai was at my side. Shorty had lowered his knife, but I was still worried that he would run Muscles down and stab him.

"Why don't you let me hold the knife?"

"What?" Shorty barked, like I had just asked for a kidney.

"You could get it from the Panther office later. Right on 122nd and Seventh Avenue."

"I know where the office is," Shorty replied. "My aunt got clothes and food there before." Shorty handed me the hunting knife and walked off.

Masai looked at me and shook his head. "Are you crazy,

Jamal? You don't jump in front of a knife like that." It was a warning and a compliment at the same time.

When I was a kid there was a neighborhood wino who we called Mr. Charlie. Now this was a funny name for a black man, since Charlie and Mr. Charlie were nicknames commonly reserved for white people. But our parents would not let us call any adult by their first name, so Charlie the wino became known to us kids as Mr. Charlie.

There were two cool things about Charlie. One, after he downed about a pint of wine and got his head where he needed it to be, he would forget we were kids and share the second pint with us. Two, he would tell us crazy stories about the Korean War. Mr. Charlie was in a black unit that saw two-thirds of its men killed in combat, and he told us he was "shell-shocked" and on full disability from the Veterans Administration. It wasn't recognized as posttraumatic stress disorder in those days, but Mr. Charlie had clearly been damaged by the war.

One story he told was about driving in a convoy at high speeds late at night with the headlights off, so Korean artillery could not get a fix on their positions. Every so often a Korean local would run in front of the truck as though he wanted to be killed. Drivers were ordered not to stop for fear of the enemy opening fire, and sometimes these people would get hit and the convoy would roll on. Mr. Charlie explained that Korean men weren't actually trying to kill themselves, but instead wanted to kill a demon that was riding on their back.

They believed the only way to do this was to have a truck barely miss them, and that would kill the demon.

As I grew into my teenage years, I began to secretly believe that a demon was on my back and that it would take a near brush with death to remove it. Not only did my demon ride me, but I believed he killed many people close to me, like Pa Baltimore; my mother, Gladys; and Panther leaders like Bunchy Carter and John Huggins who were assassinated on my birthday. A part of me believed these deaths were all my fault, as was the arrest of the Panther 21 because of the actions of Yedwa, my mentor. So I kept pushing myself into dangerous situations, hoping that those near-miss razor slashes and gunshots would kill the demon, once and for all.

The Panther office was essentially a crisis and relief center with socialist politics. People would come in at all hours to have us break up disputes, intervene when the cops were making arrests, or for emergency medical care and disputes with slumlords. A few people even kicked the heroin habit in the Panther office. We once took turns sitting with a twenty-year-old brother named Stan as for three days he sweated, shivered, cramped, and vomited. He had tried to kick the drug a couple of times before but felt that having the Panthers standing guard over him was the charm he needed to break the habit.

Drugs were an epidemic in Harlem. There were intersections and blocks where junkies would line up to buy drugs in full view of the cops and the community. In fact, many of the cops were on the drug dealers' payrolls, and the community felt powerless to do anything. We would claim certain areas as "liberated territory" and make it plain to the drug dealers that we would deal with them if they came there. Blocks where we organized buildings, breakfast programs, liberation schools, and so on were off limits.

But we knew the Panthers alone could not run all of the drug dealers from the community. It would be the community itself, strong and organized into a "people's party" and a "people's army," that would make it impossible for drugs and crime to exist. Our goal was not to have every black person in the community join the Black Panther Party but rather to make the Black Panther Party obsolete because the whole community had become politicized and organized. In our youth, fueled by enthusiasm, we truly believed this would happen. The only question was how long it would take.

One night a group of us community activists were hanging out in the dorms of Columbia University—Panthers, Students for a Democratic Society (SDS), Young Lords, Asian activists, and members of the women's movement. We got into a heavy debate about how long the revolution would take. "One year," an optimist shouted. Felipe Luciano, Denise Oliver, and Yoruba Guzman from the Lords predicted Puerto Rican independence and socialism within two years. "Five years," a pragmatist countered. Finally we agreed that the military-industrial complex of America was too difficult an enemy to overcome quickly and that the revolution would take at least ten years. This led us to the horrifying realization that those of us who lived might be near or over thirty when the people's victory arrived.

Not only was this the night that I helped to set the date for our goal of completing the revolution, it was the first time I dropped acid. An SDS kid passed out tabs of "sunshine," and I swallowed one with some wine. For a while I felt nothing. I was used to a swig of wine or a hit of a joint going to my head in a few seconds. This is some bullshit, I thought as I watched people roll around and dance in the dorm rooms. Acid must be a white-people thing, cuz I don't feel nothin'. That's when the first burst of electric butterflies exploded in my stomach and shot up my spine. "Damn," I said out loud. A few seconds later another burst. Then I started laughing uncontrollably.

"Just relax," a pretty white student named Natalie said to me. She guided me to a bed and helped me stretch out. "Just breathe and feel the music. Everything is cool." The ceiling melted away and the sky was filled with colors as Jimi Hendrix's "All Along the Watchtower" played in the background. Natalie gave me fruit, juice, hugs, and cookies and made sure I was okay as the trip got more intense. Eventually we wound up in the dorm shower together and got it on, laughing, coming up with crazy positions, slipping on soap, and falling on our asses. There was no towel so we wrapped our wet bodies under one sheet and stumbled back to her dorm bed.

As I lay next to Natalie, the vision of revolution in our life-time started playing in my head. There were rainbow people dancing in the streets; Sly and the Family Stone's "Everyday People" was the new national anthem; President Bobby Seale ordered the White House to be painted black and blue, the Panther colors. But I'm not at the celebration. Instead I'm in a grave, dead at seventeen, my troubled spirit watching every-thing from the other side. My trip suddenly made me feel that I needed to be back in Harlem, back on the street. I climbed out of bed and found my clothes. Natalie opened her eyes and smiled at me. "See you in the colors," she said. We hugged again and I left.

At three thirty, maybe four, in the morning, I'm standing on Amsterdam Avenue waiting for the light to change, or ac-tually stuck in the same spot, watching the same stoplight explode from green to yellow to red, accompanied by bursts of music. Suddenly I feel a heavy weight on my back. A swirling shadow. My demon. I run into traffic like one of the Korean men in Mr. Charlie's war stories. A taxi driver blares his horn. A truck bears down on me. I stop, frozen for a second, and then run. The truck barely misses me.

The stocky white truck driver pulls the vehicle over, hops out, and walks toward me as if he plans to kick my ass. "Are you fucking crazy? What the hell is the matter with you?"

The threat of a fight suddenly cleared my head. "Nothing's the matter with me. Why don't you watch where the fuck you're going?" I yelled as I jumped into a combat stance and threw some punches at the air.

The truck driver shook his head and climbed back in his cab. "Fuckin' psycho," he muttered as he pulled off.

I rubbed my eyes and checked the streets to see if my demon was lying dead on the asphalt. Nothing. I took a couple of deep breaths and headed down the hill toward Harlem.

Once a black teacher from a Harlem school came into the office and asked if I could come and speak to her class. I said yes and scribbled down the date on a piece of paper, then put the paper in the desk drawer and forgot about it. A couple of weeks later Afeni approached me and said that the teacher had returned to the office disappointed because I failed to show up at her class assembly. I responded about some Panther assignment that had come up that was more important. I had jumped into a car with a group of Panther officers to head up to New Haven where tension was brewing between the local police and black residents. The New Haven chapter asked for reinforcements, and I was one of the first out the door looking for "action."

"Nothing is more important than keeping your word once you've made a commitment," Afeni said, "especially when you've made a commitment to black children. Their lives are already filled with disappointments and broken promises. The least you should have done was to contact the teacher and let her know that you weren't coming."

Afeni had put me "in check," and I accepted her admonition humbly. Panthers, especially Panther men, tended to have a healthy dose of arrogance to go along with the swagger. We were badass dudes who were willing to die for our beliefs, but we could also be cocky-ass dudes who felt we could do no wrong. One of our guiding principles was respecting criticism and constructive self-criticism. Afeni would often be the first to point out our personal and our organizational mistakes, especially when it came to the community. She could give the criticism gently or ferociously, but she never held back. She could theorize with the best of the party's intellectuals and cuss with the meanest of the party's street cats. I learned many of the important lessons of manhood from Afeni. Keeping my word, loving and caring for children, respecting women as equals, and honoring and taking time for my elders were all things that she impressed upon me.

I also learned from her what quiet courage was and how it could be more effective than the loud bravado of leaping at flying bullets. One morning Afeni and I were alone in the dining room of a Harlem church where the Panthers conducted its breakfast program. The kids were gone, and I was mopping the dining room when a dozen cops with guns drawn stormed into the basement. A white lieutenant with a gold shield and a suit walked up to me.

"What's going on down here?" he asked, snarling.

"It's a community program," I snapped back. "We serve free breakfast to children."

"We got a report that someone is down here with a gun."

"Ain't no guns down here," I replied. "I told you this is a community breakfast program." I deliberately left out the word Black Panther, because it was clear that this raid was a setup. The pigs were about to arrest us or kill us and then conveniently find a gun that they would claim was a Panther weapon. We'd heard that Panther programs were being harassed and shut down in this way all across the country.

Afeni marched from the back where she was putting away cooking pans. Taking up a position between me and the cops, she turned her back on the lieutenant and spoke to me as though he wasn't even there.

"Don't say another word to him," she commanded in a firm, controlled voice.

"Is there a problem?" the lieutenant asked.

Afeni turned to the lieutenant and said with the same firm voice, "The problem is that I don't speak to police officers." She then dismissed him by walking away and wiping down tables. I followed her lead and continued to mop, ignoring the cops.

"We got a call about a gun," the lieutenant repeated. Afeni ignored him, her silence creating a wall of will between us and the cops. They would do what they came to do, but we would be no part of it. The lieutenant watched us in quiet amazement for a minute or two, then raised his hand and gestured for his men to leave. He took one last look at us and left.

I was awed by what I had just witnessed. I wanted to speak, to explain, to apologize, to understand, but only stuttered syllables came out: "Afeni, uh, uh, ah, uh."

She responded to my confusion by holding me in a tight embrace. "You're a brave brother, Jamal. I'm glad you're here with me." We finished cleaning in silence. The moment was sealed in my consciousness, the lesson of quiet strength learned.

11

The Love of the People

I was very excited when other members of the Panther 21 were finally released on bail. The Panther Defense Committee worked exhaustively to raise bail money, but one hundred thousand dollars per Panther was a lot of money. Although twenty-one New York Panthers had been indicted, only thirteen would actually stand trial. Lonnie Epps, a high school student from Queens, and I were severed from the main case because of our ages. Others had avoided capture and were living underground. Lee Berry, an army veteran suffering from severe epilepsy, was deemed medically unable to stand trial.

A dynamic member of the 21 to be released was Michael Cetewayo Tabor. Cetewayo grew up in Harlem where he was an honor student and an All-City basketball star in high school. However, he was raised in a housing project where there was an epidemic of crime and drugs, and his promising basketball career was cut short when he became addicted to heroin. Cetewayo, or Cet as we called him, kicked the drug habit and became a black nationalist. By the time he joined the Black Panther Party, he had become a brilliant self-educated black historian and political theorist. At twenty-four, he was an articulate and commanding presence with chiseled African features and a booming bass voice, reminiscent of Paul Robeson. The Panther 21 voted Cet to be the next released because of his oratory skills.

Saturdays on 125th Street were a cultural explosion. There were street vendors selling clothing, books, records, incense, food, and almost anything else you could think of. Afros, dashikis, and BLACK POWER buttons would blend with silk pants, flashy jewelry, and gangster hats, creating a vibrant sea of human black energy. Along the street there were activists and believers from dozens of cultural, political, and religious groups. Each spokesperson waved a Bible, Koran, book, newspaper, or flyer at passersby, declaring that their way was the "right way" to truth and salvation.

The main event and the main stage would be a Saturday afternoon on the corner of 125th Street and Seventh Avenue. Over time, virtually every important black leader spoke there—Marcus Garvey, Congressman Adam Clayton Powell Jr., Dr. Martin Luther King Jr., and of course Malcolm X. The Saturday afternoon crowds could range from a few dozen to a few thousand, depending on the speaker and the event. If Harlem was the black capital of the world, and 125th Street the main artery, then the corner of Seventh Avenue was its rhythmicly pulsating, energized, super-bad heart.

The Harlem Panthers would go out to that corner on Saturdays with a bullhorn and some papers and start to "blow." "Blowing" was a term borrowed from jazz musicians who could really play their instruments. A trumpet, sax, piano, or bass player would get not only applause after a dynamite solo but the compliment "Man, that cat can really blow!" The same was true for public speakers who could get to the nitty-gritty with an eloquence and passion that fired up the audience and took them on a ride.

Cet was like that—he could really blow. He would stand on the corner and start running down the Panther program, and instantly he'd draw a crowd. It was that booming voice and that mixture of sophisticated vocabulary and street slang that fired the imagination. Afeni could really blow too; she was passionate, soulful, sultry. If she were a jazz singer, she'd be somewhere between Nina Simone and Nancy Wilson:

keeping it real about the battle but never letting you forget that revolutionaries were motivated by great feelings of love.

Dhoruba had been released a few weeks earlier. He was a former gang leader from the Bronx turned visual artist, and he spent most of his teen years in prison, where he immersed himself in books, nurturing a brilliant mind. Dhoruba could blow. Whipping a crowd into a frenzy with deadly verbal jabs at racism and capitalism.

The fifth and final member of the Panther 21 to be released was Joan Bird. Soft eyes, with an even softer voice, Joan was a college nursing student who helped run the Panthers' health cadre. The previous January the cops dragged Joan from a parked car on Harlem River Drive. Someone had fired shots at a cop car from that direction. Manhandled from the outset, she was taken to a nearby precinct where she said she was slapped, punched, and kicked. The cops grabbed her by her ankles and hung her outside a third-story window for ten minutes. Torture, plain and simple, of a young black woman, not on a plantation in the deep South during slavery, but in New York City four years after the signing of the Civil Rights Act.

Joan's parents got her a lawyer and bailed her out of prison demanding that she stay away from the Panthers. She concentrated on her college classes and her court dates, only to be arrested again as part of the Panther 21 conspiracy case. "The pigs don't let you quit," Dhoruba used to say, "even if you try to walk away from the struggle. They'll never forget that you had the nerve to stand up to their tyrannical bullshit." We didn't know that Joan would be the last of the Panther 21 to be bailed out, but after that there was never enough money in the bail fund to open the gates for another comrade.

By now it was late spring and the feelings of optimism in the community were high. The freed members of the Panther 21 appeared together and separately at events all over the country. We were constantly on the road, speeding up and down the highway in one of the cars or vans that belonged to the party. Like most teenagers, I wanted to learn how to drive, especially when I witnessed the stuntlike exploits of Bullwhip (Cyril Innis) from Queens. My first driving lesson was literally on the highway where Bullwhip and John Thomas, a captain from the Panthers' Queens chapter, pulled over and let me get behind the wheel. Thirty seconds later I was in traffic, driving sixty miles an hour, with Bullwhip telling me, "Just point the car and go," and John Thomas screaming, "Watch where the fuck you're going!" Not exactly the Acme Driving School, but by the time I pulled off the highway thirty minutes later I could handle a car.

A few lessons later I was doing screeching turns and forty-mile-an-hour parallel-parking stunts, just like the older Panthers. Whenever I had the chance I would commandeer the wheel and race up the highway with a car full of Panthers, blasting James Brown, Hendrix, or "American Woman" by the Guess Who. One of my SDS friends hooked me up with a phony license. Who had the time to mess with the pigs for something legitimate?

My first airplane flight was to San Francisco to visit the Panther national headquarters in Oakland. I had butterflies as the plane took off, but I had a ball with Cet, Afeni, and Dhoruba as the plane crossed the country. The ghettos of Oakland were heaven compared with the slums of Harlem. In fact, we teased the Oakland Panthers about their petty bourgeois lifestyle. "What are ya all mad about out here? Everybody's got a house, grass, and a car," I joked. "If we could make Harlem look like Oakland, the revolution would be over tomorrow." Then we were driven to the rougher parts of the black community in Oakland and San Francisco. The buildings may not have been the cramped, crumbling high-rise projects I knew, but the oppressive living conditions were obvious.

We met with David Hilliard, the party's chief of staff; Masai; and other party leaders to talk about the Panther 21 case, in the course of which Hilliard told us about the hundreds of other cases pending against Panthers around the country. They included Panther founder Huey P. Newton, who was fighting to win his appeal on manslaughter charges, and Chairman Bobby Seale, who was facing the electric chair in Connecticut in a murder conspiracy case. We were made to understand that the party's resources were stretched thin and that some of the support for the Panther 21 needed to be placed elsewhere—not great news to us, but we understood that we were part of a war that had to be fought on many fronts.

There was a pickup truck full of sand in front of national headquarters. Panthers used the sand to fill small canvas bags that were sewn shut and stacked bunker-style inside the office. The plate-glass windows had been replaced with plywood, which was painted the party colors (black and blue). Gun portholes had been cut into the plywood. The office was being turned into a fort. I stripped down to my T-shirt and grabbed a shovel, excited that I was helping fortify our national headquarters. It never occurred to me that we might actually be building a fortified tomb for any Panther caught inside, under the barrage of police bullets.

Two days later I was back in the crumbling tenements of Harlem. The freed members of the Panther 21 had spent a lot of time together working out of the Harlem office and speaking at fund-raising events for the Panther 21. Now we were dispersed at different offices to help run daily operations and to fund-raise at events for other Panther political prisoners. Afeni was assigned to the Bronx. Dhoruba was sent to Brooklyn.

I was sent to Jersey City. The Panther headquarters there was a rented brownstone with offices on the first floor and living quarters upstairs. Jersey City had blocks of rundown houses and vacant lots as well as a low-rise housing project. The feel was a lot like South Jamaica, Queens, or West

Philadelphia, where the slums were spread out, as opposed to the congestion of Harlem or the South Side of Chicago. But the issues that we organized around were still the same: decent housing, food, and police brutality. Plus, the Jersey City cops would harass and arrest Panthers whenever they could. The headquarters was also shot at and vandalized. I ran PE classes, spoke around the community, and sold papers.

The membership in Jersey City never grew beyond twenty, but community projects like the distribution of free clothing and the breakfast program were highly successful. Actually, declining membership was a reality in most chapters. People were afraid to become full-fledged members of the Panthers, but they would come out to the programs and community meetings. Who could blame them? On television, in the papers, and before their eyes, Panthers were being beaten, arrested, and killed.

I would grab a late-night ride to Harlem once or twice a week to hang out, especially to spend time with Joan Bird. I had assigned myself to be her "security team" when she was first released from prison. I made sure she got to her speaking engagements and appointments on time, and then I'd drop her at her parents' house each evening. One evening we wound up in a Panther pad and spent the night together. Soon after, she let me know that she no longer needed a constant security detail, especially since we were just taking subways and buses to various appointments. But I was still welcome to hang out with her whenever we could make a rendezvous work.

The opening of the Panther 21 trial was fast approaching. Our lawyers worked out of a space in Union Square they called "the law commune." It consisted of open space, zigzag desks, file cabinets, and papers everywhere, thousands of pages of transcripts from tape recordings and documents crucial to our defense. Once or twice a week we would travel down to the commune to meet with the lawyers. A few weeks before the trial began the law commune went up in flames. A fire of suspicious origin began at night, destroying most of the documents. The Panthers and the lawyers had no doubt that this was arson. The police and the fire marshals basically shrugged, saying that the evidence was inconclusive.

The law commune fire added to the mounting tension among and between the Panther 21. Filling sandbags on a sunny day, or hearing hundreds of people chant "Free the Panther 21" at a midnight rock concert rally, had the effect of creating a revolutionary magic spell where anything seemed possible and victory over the oppressor was assured. But fires, office bombings, arrests, and shoot-outs brought home that we were, in reality, under siege.

The lawyers fought with the judge and got him to grant permission for the bailed-out members of the 21 to go back into prison for conference visits with those still imprisoned. Among the charges against us was a long indictment that cited meetings, conversations, and training sessions that we were all a part of. How could we defend ourselves unless we could compare our own recollections against the allegations in the indictment? The meetings were held in the Branch Queens House of Detention in Long Island City, usually in a small conference room or in the prison chapel. We would discuss the case, then huddle in smaller groups to talk about what was happening in the party.

One of the biggest beefs Lumumba and the other comrades on the inside had was that bail money was being diverted to other Panther cases. They felt that we on the outside should be fighting harder to protect every dollar being raised so that it could be used for the Panther 21. We explained that some fund-raising events were dedicated to the Panther 21, but other events were for a general Panther defense fund. This led to beef number two, which was that we should be spending all of our time raising money for the Panther 21. "Not possible," we responded. "We are part of a national movement that is fighting on many fronts. Everybody out there is working eighteen to twenty-one hours a day to help keep it together."

Beef number three: A number of New York Panthers, including the wives and relatives of the Panther 21, had been disciplined or even suspended from the party by California Panthers who had been transferred to New York to assume leadership positions. There was some truth to this complaint. The bailed-out members of the 21 had spent a lot of time battling bad decisions and the prevailing belief that New York and every other chapter should be run exactly like Oakland. At first these jailhouse meetings would end on a positive note. We would leave with strategies and proposals for making things in the party better. But as time went on, a rift between Panther 21 members on the inside and those outside the prison developed. Not many of the suggestions made by 21 members on the inside were implemented. There was also frustration that Panther 21 members on the outside were too busy with national issues to give their full attention to helping the lawyers and the imprisoned members prepare for the upcoming trial.

None of the Panthers still "inside" were content to sit in their prison cells waiting for visits, letters from the outside, or trips to the enclosed prison roof to play basketball. They were organizers, agitators, and revolutionaries to the nth degree. Whoever they encountered was transformed. Fellow prisoners were passed books and newspapers and given on-the-spot political education classes. Social workers, chaplains, and guards all caught an earful about the contradiction in the legal system that was designed to protect the rich and persecute the poor.

Dr. King, Medgar Evers, Fannie Lou Hamer, and Malcolm X had left a legacy that taught us to organize people around their common needs and interest. In Montgomery, Alabama, it was a bus boycott around the issue of transportation. In

Mississippi it was schools and the right to vote. In Oakland, California, it was Panthers with shotguns and law books organizing to challenge police brutality. In New York, Philly, Chicago, and other Panther chapters it was housing, poverty, and poor children going to school hungry that fired the engine. In Branch Queens, Lumumba and the other Panther prisoners would organize the prisoners around the issue of a fair trial and reasonable bail.

After weeks of teaching and organizing in small groups, the Branch Queens Panthers led a swift and explosive takeover of the prison. Riot doesn't describe what happened, because the Panthers and prisoners took control of the building so quickly the guards never knew what hit them. They used the prison telephones to call lawyers and the press, and within hours a vigil was set up outside the prison where hundreds of people stayed to ensure that there would be no brutality or reprisals. A stage was erected in front of the prison. Afeni, Dhoruba, and I spoke to the crowd, who demanded the release of all prisoners. Gerry Lefcourt, Bob Bloom, and the other lawyers helped the Panthers negotiate with the prison and the courts. They demanded and received bail hearings for every prisoner. Judges came to Branch Queens and other prisons and held hearings to review bad bail decisions. As a result, hundreds of prisoners were released.

The Panthers managed to break out the bars in their unit so they had a clear view of the street. The final triumphant part of the negotiation was that a cherry picker lowered them from their windows into prison vans, which then safely transported them without fear of reprisal to another prison. The fact that the rebellion was used to point out class and racial inequities in the system was a first in the history of U.S. prison rebellions. The usual demands were for better food and living conditions, but the imprisoned members of the Panther 21 knew that this was a bigger moment and that their case and celebrity could be used to make an immediate as well as long-term impact. The sight of Panther 21 members riding down in those cherry pickers with clenched fists was the equivalent of watching Hannibal entering Rome.

The day after the Panther 21 descended victoriously in the cherry picker, I went home to the Bronx to see Noonie. I felt like a young soldier on leave after a long military campaign. I had tried to remember to call her at least once a week but often failed to do this. Now seemed like the right time to visit. Her home-cooked meal of stewed chicken and rice was the best food I'd had in months. She sat across from me at the kitchen table and watched me eat with a smile. When I was younger I used to cut off her loving looks with a "What?" or "Noonie, don't stare. You're the one who told me that's not nice." But this time I pretended not to notice. I knew she missed her Eddie terribly and that my absence, albeit for the cause, was lonely and painful for her.

After dinner I went downstairs and hung out on the stoop

with my childhood best friends, John Danavall, Roy Campbell, and Darryl Tookes. We talked about girls and guys from the neighborhood, basketball, and college. College was a distant and foreign thought to me. I was home from the revolutionary battlefield, and the best I could do in this conversation was to urge them to be radical students, wherever they wound up. I was surprised how much the fellas knew about the Panthers and the Panther 21 case. They had news clippings about me I hadn't seen. They were proud of me but also worried. I shrugged it off with a couple of revolutionary quotes about "the people's victory over oppression." Walking around the neighborhood with them was a trip. The old folks would greet me with "Are you saying out of trouble, boy?" or "You know we're praying for you." The girls we used to mess with would either come over and flirt, asking about Panther meetings, or they would cross the street, saying, "I'm not gonna mess with you, Eddie Joseph. You are crazy!"

We wound up at Roy's house, listening to him playing trumpet alongside his father's jazz records. Darryl started playing chords on the piano and scatting. I had no idea then that within a few years Roy and Darryl would become accomplished and world-famous musicians. Roy would be a sideman to many jazz greats and would become a respected band leader and composer in his own right. Darryl would sing, play, and arrange for everyone from Roberta Flack to Michael Jackson and become a well-known pop, rock, jazz, and funk icon. John would spend time in Africa, working in music promotion and distribution, and return to America to work as a counselor and educator.

That evening I was back home by eleven, respecting Noonie's curfew. I climbed into bed and slept for fifteen straight hours. The comfort of home let my body relax in a way that was impossible on old beat-up mattresses in a Panther pad or a sleeping bag on the floor of the Panther office. I was in a dreamlike daze when I stepped outside the next day. I hadn't rested like that in months. The feeling of a good night's sleep was so foreign to my body that the experience was like being high. I sat on the stoop watching children coming home from school, playing tag and catch, and jumping rope on this safe, quiet black working-class block in the Bronx. Harlem and the Panther office were just a forty-minute subway ride away, but these worlds couldn't have been more different.

I wondered what it would be like if I just stayed. If I called the Panther office and said, "I'm not coming back." Or just didn't show up. Noonie and my friends still loved me. My bed was still warm. The home-cooked meals were still good.

Then I thought about the slums, the hungry kids, the racist cops, and I started to feel like I was sitting in a bubble. Most black folks didn't live like this. I got anxious. I knew it was time to go. I went upstairs, hugged Noonie, and jumped on the subway headed back to 125th Street.

12

A Moment of Doubt

Summer 1970. I had been out of prison for four months. It felt like a year. Constantly in motion. Doing public speaking; conducting political education classes and leadership meetings; taking part in community patrols; cooking breakfast for kids; hitting rats with a shovel while trying to clean garbage out of an alley; sitting in the hospital with brothers who had their skulls cracked by the police; watching people die in the gutter from drugs, bullets, and stab wounds; watching sick babies cry in their mothers' arms.

All this was intensified by the summer's blazing heat, the smell of sweaty bodies on the street, the stench of rotting garbage mingled with incense from street vendors, and music everywhere. Record shops with blaring speakers, African drummers playing on stops and park benches, jazz and R&B clubs with doors flung wide open. And every so often there was the sound of sirens—the through line to the sound track of revolution. I would stand on the corner of 125th Street and Seventh Avenue and take it all in.

That's where I was when I got the news. The Panthers from the office ran up to me shouting that Huey P. Newton was free. We hugged, pumped our fists, and practically danced up and down 125th Street, handing out flyers and spreading the word. Later we gathered in the Panther office to watch the news on television. Huey stepped out of prison and climbed on top of a car to greet hundreds of supporters who had gathered. He ripped off his prison shirt and threw his arms up in victory. Huey had a body builder's physique, and with his outstretched arms he looked like an Olympic champion, a conquering warrior, a Panther Adonis ready to lead the oppressed masses to victory and freedom.

We were energized beyond measure by Huey's release. It was lightning in our veins, rockets on our feet. Panthers always had a certain swagger when they walked—part cat, part sexual god, three parts bad motherfucker. Man, did we get our swagger on in the community and in the face of the police, just thinking about how the movement would grow now that Huey was free.

At his first press conference, Huey promised to send a regiment of Black Panthers to Vietnam to fight alongside the North Vietnamese people. I pictured myself in the jungle, wearing sandals and black ninjalike pajamas, carrying an AK47 rifle. Then he talked about meeting with revolutionary leaders from Cuba, North Korea, and China to organize a revolutionary tribunal that would try President Nixon and the U.S. government for war crimes. I pictured myself in a Mao-style jacket, accompanying Huey as part of the Panther Diplomatic Delegation. Whatever the assignment from Huey, I was ready to serve.

A few weeks later Huey came to Harlem. He had said that Harlem was the black capital of the world and that he was moving the national headquarters of the Black Panther Party there, and to that end the Panthers had purchased a large brownstone on 127th Street. It needed a lot of improvement, and we took turns working shifts on the renovation. The building was also to serve as Huey's residence in New York. Huey came to the office with David Hilliard and other Panther leaders. He shook our hands, embraced us, and talked to us about the work we had to do to free Bobby Seale, the Panther 21, and all political prisoners.

Then we walked through Harlem. A crowd gathered and followed us everywhere. There was Huey on 125th Street. That corner where all the great leaders stood. My corner. The day ended at a nice large apartment downtown where Huey was a guest. I sat on the floor of the living room filled with the radical-chic leftist intellectuals and Panther elite and listened to Huey speak about his new theories, and discourse on the lumpen proletariat revolution, and "Intercommunicalism"— an evolved form of Marxism.

I came back to the Panther pad in the wee hours of the morning excited about Harlem's future with our leader in residence, but Huey never returned. Work on the house on 127th Street was never completed, and within a year COINTELPRO, the FBI's Counter Intelligence Program, would create a deep divide and bitter split between the East Coast and West Coast chapters of the Black Panther Party.

The trial of the Panther 21, who now numbered thirteen, began on September 8, 1970. Because of my age, my trial had been severed, and I would be tried separately. Before opening arguments could be made, a jury had to be selected. Our defense strategy was to point out the contradictions in the American justice system by fighting for a jury that truly represented the Panthers' peer group. The Panthers' preference would have been to hold the trial in Harlem, perhaps at the Apollo, with nooses on the stage and a jury of brothers and sisters off the block who could see the case for the attempt at legal lynching it really was. The next best thing would be to have that Harlem jury downtown, a jury that would comprise

artists, ex-convicts, recovering drug addicts, veterans, teachers, transit workers, community organizers, students, young
women, a computer engineer, and one African American man
with a PhD in biology—a jury that truly reflected the lives
and occupations of the Panther 21.

The Manhattan jury pool comprised mainly white male
registered voters. The jury-selection process disqualified or
eliminated most of the black, poor, and disenfranchised can-
didates who could be considered true peers of the majority of
black defendants who went to trial in New York. Many black
men in prison were sitting there because of white judges and
white juries. The Panther 21 decided to use the jury-selection
process to point out the contradictions in the system. Judge
John Murtagh and Assistant District Attorney Joseph Phillips
would have loved to seat the jury in one day so that the justice railroad train could leave the station immediately, but the
Panthers and our attorneys were not having it.

Jury selection is a chess game. Both sides get to question
prospective jurors. If either the prosecution or the defense does
not like a juror, it tries to get the judge to dismiss that person for "cause." A paralegal who worked for civil rights causes
would be challenged by the prosecution. A woman whose son
was a police officer would be challenged by the defense. Other
challenges based on political or religious beliefs or perceived
prejudices were harder to argue. If one side could not get a
juror dismissed for cause, then it could use one of its twelve

preemptory challenges. The selection process in the Panther 21 trial continued for weeks, with lots of questions coming from our side about the civil rights movement, the Vietnam War, and the black-power struggle. There were heated fights with the judge, and when challenges were exhausted we finally had a jury of twelve, including four African Americans, four women, and a black jury foreman, Clarence Fox.

The prosecution's opening arguments talked about bomb plots, hatred, and seized weapons that were intended for use in an all-out guerrilla war against the police and the government. The defense's opening argument was about the history of slavery, dehumanization, the civil rights movement, and black people's constitutional right to bear arms as self-defense against racist members of society who in the past had beaten, lynched, burned, bombed, and murdered people of color.

The typical relationship between a poor person on trial and his attorney is that of the common versus the elite. The lawyer is a sorcerer who understands the wizardry that is the law. The defendant is the commoner, unfortunate enough to be in the clutches of the empire but lucky to have a sorcerer willing to donate a bit of precious time to his case. No need for the commoner to ask questions about the process, because it's too complex for him to understand. And how dare the commoner question the strategy or the actions of the wizard. If the commoner had a grasp of how the law worked, he wouldn't be in this miserable situation to begin with.

The relationship between the Panthers and their attorneys was quite different. The energy was that of comrades struggling together in a battle that might be lost, but one that would be remembered for the ages. The lawyers respected the intelligence, commitment, and perspective of the Panthers. They saw us not as victims but as targets, people who were being persecuted and prosecuted because they had a well-developed ideology and a clear sense of direction. Advice was given, debates were had, but the lawyers always deferred to the Panthers as to what the courtroom strategy would be.

A few days into the trial the judge ordered a morning recess. When court resumed an hour later, court officers blocked my way and informed me that the judge had banned me from the courtroom. I, of course, made a scene, talking about my constitutional rights to witness a public hearing and trying to push my way past the guards. The lawyers went to talk to Judge Murtagh who confirmed that he granted the prosecution's request that I not be allowed in the court. Since I was still a defendant I should not be allowed to observe witnesses and evidence that would be used against me. It was a ridiculous decision, but the judge held his fascist ground. Later I learned that the prosecutor didn't want the baby-faced Panther in the second row influencing the jury as I made eye contact and exchanged smiles and clenched fists with the Panthers on trial.

I felt angry and helpless, further severed from the battles and fate of my Panther 21 comrades. I would see Afeni, Dhoruba, Cet, and Joan each day as they dragged into the Panther office after court, mad, weary, and tense, like fighters in the seventh round of a brutal fifteen-round match. We would debrief on the run, each of us headed to a meeting, a fund-raiser, a building in crisis, or a corner where the police were shoving people. There was no time for them really to unwind.

Besides the battle in court with the prosecution, there was the battle with the Panthers in prison. Harsh words and cold feelings were the communication between those on the inside and those out on bail. These were the same issues that had been in place for months: frustration over the lack of success in bailing all the Panthers out, concern that Panthers were spending more time selling papers and less time in community programs, and a national leadership that was perceived as being insensitive to the needs and suggestions of rank-and-file members. One morning, Judge Murtagh threw Cet in jail because he was an hour late for court. He had the flu and a bronchitis attack, but no matter to Murtagh. He did the same to Afeni one morning because she was a few minutes late. The lawyers objected strenuously, and Afeni and Cet's bail were restored by the end of the day. Judge Murtagh saw he had leverage over all of the Panthers when it came to bail. He threatened to take away everyone's bail if there were any more outbursts or contempt of court behavior by the Panthers or their attorneys.

One night, near the Bronx Panther office, Afeni pulled me to the side and told me she was pregnant. Her husband, Lumumba, had been in prison for sixteen months.

"Lumumba?" I asked, thinking maybe they had been able to steal an intimate moment together during a prison visit. Even as I asked, I knew it was impossible. Prison security on the Panthers was always extremely tight, especially after the Branch Queens prison rebellion.

"No," she said. "Not Lumumba." She offered no details and I didn't ask. All that mattered was to comfort her and hold dear the secret that my big sister Afeni was sharing.

"What are you going to do?" I asked.

"I'm telling Lumumba," Afeni answered, "and I'm keeping the baby. I didn't think I could conceive, and it feels wrong to even think about ending this life. I know they're going to give me three hundred years, and I know it's crazy, but if I can pass something of my spirit on to this child, maybe the struggle will continue."

Afeni's sister, Gloria Jean, wasn't a Panther but loved and supported Afeni with all of her being. Gloria Jean would take good care of Afeni's baby along with her own children. My worry was about Afeni when she told Lumumba. The principled, rigorous, sometimes fearsome Panther captain, who treasured duty over life, might take her out right in the courtroom.

"Maybe you should wait," I counseled.

"No, I have to tell him," Afeni replied.

A few days later Afeni broke the news to Lumumba in the courtroom. After some tense heated moments, a cold veil dropped over Lumumba. He pronounced "I divorce thee" three times, as is the custom and procedure in Islamic law. Afeni and Lumumba Shakur were no longer husband and wife. They sat near each other for the remainder of the trial, but they barely spoke to each other after that.

The prosecutors spent the first few weeks of the trial introducing the pistols, shotguns, and rifles that had been seized from Panther homes during the predawn raids. Firing pins had been taken out of the weapons to render them harmless, but it was a serious arsenal piled high on the table, left for the jury to gaze at for the duration of the trial. The prosecution's point was that the Panthers were "armed to the teeth" and had been days away from an attack. Afeni and Cet would cross-examine the cops with questions about police brutality and the wanton murder of black people. After a parade of cops, who talked about surveillance operation and photos, and hours of listening to barely audible tapes of conversations between Panthers, the two star witnesses arrived.

Gene Roberts had been part of the police department's undercover unit, BOSS—Bureau of Special Services—for several years. After infiltrating the Nation of Islam and serving as Malcolm X's bodyguard, he joined a Harlem black nationalist organization known as the Mau Mau and then the Panthers.

Gene was a navy veteran and helped to teach weapons classes. He made several trips to Maryland with Panthers to buy weapons. Gene testified about being present at secret meetings where Panthers talked about guerrilla warfare. As a witness, Gene was bland, vague, and robotic. The only time he came to life is when he talked about Malcolm X.

Then came Yedwa, wild-eyed and energetic, with a volatility that could not be suppressed by the witness stand. He was the spark the prosecution needed, the animated undercover cop who heroically leaped into the Panthers' jaws of death. Afeni stood before him, pregnant and seemingly vulnerable, and dismantled his testimony and his character.

"You testified that you were a Panther and a police officer?" Afeni asked.

"That's right," Yedwa replied.

"So, when you seduced young women in the Black Panther Party, were you being a Panther or a cop?" Afeni pressed on, hammering Yedwa about smoking marijuana, firing guns, and his erratic behavior that often created confrontations between Panthers and police. But the jury looked impassive, seemingly unmoved by the political theater and the courtroom drama happening before them. Because quiet juries are usually thought of as convicting juries, not much hope came out of the Panther 21 courtroom, even on days when the Panthers and their lawyers scored some clear points.

The war on the streets was escalating. Not a day went by

when somewhere in the country a Panther wasn't arrested or killed. There were police raids and bombings. In New York and several other cities, Panther offices were broken into and the food for the breakfast program was destroyed. "Who does that?" I asked no one in particular as I looked at the pancake and cereal mixture that had been spilled and trampled on. "A vile, fascist, cowardly pig," I answered as young Panthers around me nodded in agreement. That's when I ordered the Harlem and Bronx offices be sandbagged the same way as the national headquarters in Oakland. We set up a twenty-four-hour security schedule where armed Panthers sat by gun portals waiting for the pigs to come. It was suicide, of course, and exactly how the cops wanted us to respond.

More troubling than the certainty of a deadly police raid were the rumors that were circulating in the party that Panthers were disappearing and being killed on the orders of other Panthers. These were things spoken of in whispers, often told by Panthers who were fugitives, passing like shadows in the night, but it was enough to fuel the general feeling of distrust and paranoia. The jailed members of the Panther 21 wrote an open letter critical of the Black Panther Party. Most of the criticism was focused on Huey Newton and the party's Central Committee. The Central Committee responded by expelling the Panther 21. This created a rift between a number of chapters on the West Coast and some on the East Coast. Word was received that several freed members of the Panther 21, including myself, had been marked for death.

One night Huey P. Newton spoke at Yale University, and I was part of his security team, which was a mix of East Coast and West Coast Panthers. Huey spoke to hundreds of students and supporters who crowded into the auditorium. Then we left the auditorium through a side door, stepping into the chilly New Haven night as we escorted Huey toward a waiting car. A young white photographer slipped on a patch of ice and his camera's flash went off. The Panthers reacted to the noise and the flash by pulling their weapons. I looked around and saw a few guns pointed in the direction of the frightened photographer. The other guns were pointed at other Panthers, with New York and California Panthers ready to shoot it out in an Ivy League alley.

We recovered, put our guns away, and got Huey into the backseat of his car. Other Panthers hopped into their escort vehicles, and the caravan departed. I was behind the wheel of a rented car with Cet and his wife, Connie Matthews, who was a confidante of Huey's. We were supposed to rendezvous with Huey at a wealthy supporter's home in Connecticut. Instead I drove to a Panther safe house in Harlem. The decision was made that tonight would be the night that we'd all go underground. We changed into disguises, cut our hair, put on hats and glasses, put fake ID into our wallets, executing pieces of a plan that had been worked on for months.

"Do Afeni and Joan know?" I asked as I checked my gun and prepared to head to another location.

"Everybody knows," was the response.

Latin music from the neighbor's radio woke me up the next morning. I was in the tiny apartment of a Panther supporter in the Dominican section of Washington Heights. My back ached from the lumpy couch. I showered, found some corn flakes and not-quite-sour milk, and ate. I turned on the kitchen radio and found the soul station. I didn't blast it, lest I give away my location as a brother hiding out in a Dominican building. Plus my ears were focused as I listened for the footsteps of cops searching. The half-hour news came on, headlined with a story about fugitive Panthers. I dropped my spoon and leaned closer. The reporter talked about warrants having been issued for Dhoruba and Cet because they failed to show up for court. Then he said Afeni and Joan had been thrown in prison and their bail was remanded. Bullshit, I thought. Everybody knew. I paced the apartment confused, stressed, pissed. I put on my glasses and my doofus hat and ventured outside to buy a paper. I came back, sat on the living room floor, and began to read. Afeni Shakur and Joan Bird: bail revoked because two of the codefendants had fled.

That night I rendezvoused with other Panthers. No one could satisfactorily explain what went wrong. How the women walked into the courtroom, into a trap. I lay on the lumpy couch of the Washington Heights apartment, a gun under my pillow, feeling like hell that Afeni and Joan were back in jail, and even worse that there was nothing I could do about it.

13

Taking It to the Streets

As a young Panther I would hear stories about Eldridge Cleaver, Field Marshal Don Cox (DC), and other Panther leaders who had gone underground. I had romantic visions of them living in ghetto command centers stocked with books, food, weapons, and maps of future missions. They would don disguises and head out into the night to survey and plan the epic battles that would liberate the oppressed black communities. Then Eldridge and DC managed to slip out of the country to Algeria and Cuba, so I imagined them living in guarded villas or jungle training camps with other fugitive Panthers, preparing for battle.

My journey to the underground was neither romantic nor sexy. I kept moving from rundown tenements to dank basement apartments, always looking over my shoulder or lying awake, expecting the cops to show up with guns blazing. I got messages by making calls from a phone booth at prearranged times to other phone booths. My Panther comrades told me that the cops were tearing up the Bronx and Harlem looking for Dhoruba, Cet, and me. We laid low while we waited for our white radical friends to get us passports and plane tickets to leave the country. Some fugitive Panthers had made their way to Cuba for asylum. Some even hijacked jets from Miami to Cuba. The Cuban government frowned on this development and established a treaty with the United States regarding hijackers. When some fugitive Panthers reported they no longer felt welcome in Cuba, the migration for Panthers in exile followed Eldridge Cleaver to Algeria.

By then, a staggering divide had developed between Panthers on the West Coast headquartered in Oakland, California, and Panthers on the East Coast headquartered in Harlem, with the Panther 21 at the center of the controversy. Huey's writings and speeches became more Marxist intellectual. He began to talk more about Panther community programs and political reform. East Coast Panthers began throwing their loyalty to Eldridge Cleaver, who continued preaching armed revolution and the violent overthrow of the government. Eldridge's appeal to rank-and-file Panthers also came from the feeling that local offices and jailed Panthers from those chapters were not receiving financial and logistical support from national headquarters. This dissension was further fueled by forged letters, documents, and anonymous phone calls the FBI created as part of its counterintelligence program. Both Huey and Eldridge received these manufactured death threats, implying that each leader was out to kill the other.

After Huey expelled the Panther 21 from the party, Eldridge Cleaver, who was now headquartered in Algeria, called Huey in Oakland to discuss the situation. The conversation disintegrated into insults and threats. The Panther leaders hung up on each other, and the East Coast/West Coast split became official. Most West Coast chapters remained loyal to Huey. New York, Connecticut, New Jersey, Pennsylvania, and most East Coast chapters followed Eldridge.

The East Coast Panthers began publishing their own version of the Panther newspaper, *Right On*. There were territorial battles surrounding the newspaper that resulted in Panthers being killed in Harlem and Queens. It seemed bizarre and unbelievable that the movement was deteriorating so rapidly and so bitterly. From my hiding place in a Bronx basement apartment, I imagined the FBI, CIA, and cops across the country popping champagne corks and celebrating that the Panthers were fighting one another. And I was powerless to do anything; I was on the run with less than a hundred dollars to my name.

A week later I got word that a way had been made for me to get out of the country and to Algeria. The plan was to take a train to Montreal, pick up a fake passport, then catch a French airline to Algeria via Paris. A young sister from the movement posed as my girlfriend, and we acted like students on our way to Quebec for holiday. We had no weapons, but I was still nervous as hell as the conductor and customs agent checked my ticket and my fake driver's license. Once in Canada I stayed in a rooming house in Quebec that catered to West Indian immigrants. Snow was piled high and I felt somewhat safe in my bundled-up disguise as I trudged around town.

A few days later a couple of young radical Canadian students came by the rooming house with passports for us. They belonged to American soldiers in Germany, who lent them to the movement. I was given the passport of a young soldier who slightly resembled me. It wouldn't stand up under close scrutiny, but the theory was that all blacks looked alike to white people and that once I was on the plane I would be home free to Paris and Algeria. Once I got to Algerian customs I would announce I was a member of the Black Panther Party seeking political asylum. The Algerians would take me into custody, search me, detain me, question me, and lock me up for a day or two. Then someone from the Panther headquarters that had been established in Algeria would appear, vouch for me, and I would be released. I would become a young revolutionary in exile, beyond the reach of the imperialist clutches of Babylon.

I looked at the passport for a long time, picturing myself holding court with other Panthers who had made it to Cuba, Africa, China, and Algeria and traveling as a delegate of black liberation to North Vietnam, North Korea, and Cuba. Some of the fugitive Panthers I had met had become fluent in Arabic, Chinese, even Vietnamese—citizens of the revolutionary world. Some had multicultural wives. That could be me! I thought, for a moment. Then I thought about Afeni, Joan, and the rest of the Panther 21 still in jail. I thought about the young Panthers I left behind who were doing their best to keep the tattered Harlem office open. Guilt, anger, and uncertainty hit me like a wave of nausea, knowing that some of my young comrades in Harlem would get killed while I lived in exile. I would be a punk if I ran for safety while leaving everybody else behind. And in my mind, a punk was still the worst thing on the manhood-rating scale. I handed the passport back. "I'm not going," I said. "I want to roll back down to Harlem and fight."

The next day I got off the train in Grand Central Station and blended into the crowd. I took the subway to Seventy-second Street and went to the Hotel Alamac that was serving as dorm rooms for City College. I knocked on the door of a

Panther in training named Richard Lomax. He was a couple of years older than I was and had been my pledge brother in the Order of the Feather fraternity. His eyes almost popped out of his head when he saw me.

"They said you were in Cuba or Africa, Jamal."

"Get your coat and come with me right now," I ordered. "I can't answer any questions."

Richard had joined the Panthers during the eleven months that I was in prison; I had been surprised to see him at a Panther rally when I returned. Richard had always been the petit bourgeois, shirt-and-tie, college-bound kid when we were younger. I was a little unsettled by his newfound militancy and had told my fellow Panthers that I wasn't quite sure about Richard. But at least his dorm room wasn't under surveillance and I needed someone to walk into the Panther office and deliver a message. I waited down the block while Richard went into the office to retrieve some money. I gave him exactly four minutes to return. When five minutes passed I left and found refuge at an apartment of a sister named Janet Cyril, a dynamic organizer who had left the party to do more community organizing a few months earlier. I later found out that Richard was an undercover cop and that he had joined the Panthers hoping to use his relationship with me to further penetrate the organization.

Dhoruba was also hiding out in New York. He didn't make the initial trip to Canada because he was told that there were no passports and therefore no clear route to Algeria for him. Instead he should wait until a route could be created. This felt like more intrigue and suspicious promises to us. We were also hearing rumors about tensions between the international section of the Black Panther Party and the Algerian government. Panthers in Algeria might be thinking about switching asylum to North Korea or North Vietnam. The life of a revolutionary exile was looking much more problematic and not nearly so romantic.

But at home, on the streets of black America, things kept getting worse. Picture blocks of abandoned tenements and crumbling buildings, with junkies scurrying in and out of vacant apartments and brick and garbage strewn alleys to buy and use drugs. These were the drug zones of Harlem, the Bronx, and Brooklyn. Drug dealers would take over apartments, using some for sales and many others for dope dens called shooting galleries. A junkie could buy a bag of dope and then go across the hall to shoot drugs in one of the rooms furnished with broken-down couches or discarded mattresses. Before the drugs were sold in the dens, they were prepared in other apartments known as factories.

Armed street soldiers stood guard while naked women and men, wearing nothing but surgical masks, mixed the pure heroin with quinine and measured it out into glassine envelopes that sold for two, three, or five dollars. Thirty envelopes bound together represented a "bundle." Three hundred envelopes were a "load," and so on through the ounce, pound, and kilo levels. The envelopes would be sealed with a certain color tape or be stamped with a name that represented the brand of a particular dealer or crew.

Gold tape meant the drugs were coming from "Goldfinger," a black gangster who adopted the name of the James Bond movie. "Country Boys" meant they were coming from Alabama. Tens of thousands of poison envelopes on the street; thousands of junkies who would beg, hustle, and steal for a fix; millions of dollars to fund the fine clothes, flashy cars, and luxurious homes of the drug dealers. They, of course, were the well-dressed puppets of the white mobs, corrupt police, military, and governments, those who truly profited from the drug trade.

The Panthers talked about CIA-owned Air America and the drug cargo it transported out of the Golden Triangle. These profits funded mercenary groups, militias, assassinations, and other CIA covert operations. This kind of talk from the Panthers on street corners and in prison cells, union halls, and college classrooms further infuriated government officials and made them more determined to obliterate the Black Panther Party. Yet this kind of awareness and analysis also made it harder to watch the disintegration of Harlem and the Bronx because of the drug epidemic brought on with government assistance and encouragement.

Put faces on those junkies, lives in those watery, desperate eyes. Black men who in another place and time could have been soldiers, could have been warriors, scholars, architects. Black women who could be, should be, teachers, doctors, lawyers. Teenagers who should be dancing, dating, sporting with eyes that are red from studying late, as opposed to eyes that are dying from chasing a heroin date. The crumbling buildings abandoned by slumlords had stories: babies, in diapers, running from apartment to apartment into the loving arms of extended families, and rent parties where fried fish and greens were served for a dollar a plate, and soul music played while Grandma or Auntie laughed and stacked enough dollars to stave off eviction for one more month. Staircases where first kisses were shared and dreams of the future, perhaps away from the ghetto, blossomed. Those were the ghosts of the not-so-distant past and the demons of the present that we underground Panthers saw as we walked those crumbling streets among the living dead.

Dhoruba and I stood on the corner of 116th Street and Eighth Avenue where fifty, maybe a hundred, junkies flitted about buying drugs and running into the shooting galleries in full view of the community, with cops avoiding the area or ignoring it as they rode by in squad cars with payoffs in the glove compartment. "The police are an occupying army," I said in street-corner speeches not far from this junkie gathering spot. "They are not here to protect us but to protect the interest of the capitalist suppressors. That's why when a grandmother calls the cops to say someone is breaking into her house, the cops take an hour to come, if they show up at all. And that's why when a white store owner on 125th Street calls and says there's a black man outside who looks like he's *thinking* about robbing the store, the cops are on the scene before the store owner can hang up the phone."

A grandmother told us about this corner. She had raised her kids, her grandkids, and a dozen of the neighborhood kids on this block. Now she couldn't walk down it because of the drug traffic. The whole scene made us mad. Seeing the teenage girl who had probably sold her body to score the fix that she was buying confirmed our mission. We no longer called ourselves Panthers. The split between the East Coast "New York Panthers" and the West Coast "California Panthers" made the whole thing too confusing and, in my mind, irrelevant. Rather than argue with black people about which faction of the Black Panther Party to follow, we needed to be talking about the path to revolution. We considered ourselves Black Liberation Army soldiers who needed to continue to fight for freedom. As Panthers, we helped organize community marches and protests at known drug locations. The idea was to shame and intimidate drug dealers by the power of community action. The targeted drug spots would always close and change locations within a day or two. There were also more than a few beat-downs and guns drawn as Panthers made it clear to drug dealers that no poison would be sold on corners near Panther offices or churches and community centers that had Panther support.

As fugitives, we could not stand in the street with a bull-horn flanked by grandmothers and children denouncing drug dealers. Instead we chose to engage in "armed propaganda"—close the drug dens by force, and put fear in the drug dealers as they wondered which one of their drug spots would be hit next.

Drug den number one: Four of us in a car sitting across the street from a semi-abandoned tenement. It's early afternoon. Late spring. Some people on the street, but not too many. We pull the car around the corner, just out of sight of the drug den. We check our weapons—pistols, a sawed-off shotgun, an M-1 carbine with a collapsible stop. We leave the car. Guns concealed under our three-quarter army fatigue and leather jackets. We enter the building. Falling plaster and gaping holes in the floor.

Brother Brick knocks on the door of the first-floor apartment. The rest of us press ourselves against the wall on either side of the door. He'd sniffed some black pepper while we were in the car so his nose would be running and his eyes would be red—like a junkie, sick with flulike symptoms and stomach cramps, in need of a fix. "Give me two," Brother Brick says, holding out a crumpled bunch of singles when the dealer cracks the door. That's all the space we need to kick the door in and throw the dealer to the ground. "Oh shit," a black woman junkie says as we spread out through the tiny apartment in military formation.

There are two dealers inside and several junkies nodding or shooting up. "Everybody down," we command, helping people into prone positions with firm shoves. A dealer starts to reach for a gun on a table. I swing a sawed-off shotgun around. "You want to die for this poison today, brother?" I ask with the barrel inches away from his face. His eyes grow big, complimenting the size of the steely black pipe that has a 12-gauge round waiting on the other side. He shakes his head no. I shove him to the floor and help to scoop the bags of heroin laid out on a coffee table with a cracked mirror top. "Drugs are genocide," we yell to the junkies and dealers. "Stop dealing this poison or face the wrath of the people." Moments later we are on the street ripping open the dope bags and dumping the contents into the sewer.

A small crowd had gathered: a few grandmothers, kids, folks from the community. "We're shutting this drug den down," we announced. "The community needs to form a people's army to stand vigilant against drugs, police brutality, and all forms of oppression. Power to the people." The kids were wide-eyed. The grandmothers and parents applauded as we walked around the corner, jumped into our car, and sped away.

"What are the guns about?" my childhood pastor, Reverend Lloyd, asked me a few months earlier when I visited Trinity

Baptist Church in an attempt to start a free breakfast program. "The guns are not about killing people," I answered. "It's about trying to inflict a political consequence. Sixteen million armed black people means that racism will be bad for business, because those sixteen million will also be politically armed and understand that white people are not the enemy but that the institutions of oppression are. That's how we'll fight. Disrupt the capitalist system. Storm the banks and shut down the corporations. Make it bad for business to be a racist oppressor."

Reverend Lloyd didn't allow me to start the breakfast program at his church. I probably should have said the guns were just for self-defense, and then only in the most extreme cases. But the Black Panther Party's courageous—some say "crazy"—stance against the police brought issues of police brutality into the national spotlight. Even if people didn't agree with the way the Panthers used guns, ideology, and in-your-face revolutionary rhetoric to confront the police, they questioned the way the armed state responded to the Panthers, and this created protests, inquiries, and a larger conversation about human rights and political oppression in general.

As underground soldiers, we worked to make drug dealing, which we saw as a form of "ill legitimate capitalism," bad for business. We hit drug dealers in the Bronx and Harlem, flushing the drugs down toilets and sewers, taking the money we found and giving it to grassroots community programs as well as to grandmothers and activists in the neighborhood who were helping to raise the village. A bounty was put on our heads—fifty thousand to a hundred thousand dollars, according to friends who were part of the hustling night life. The drug dealers were tired of these black militants who were fucking up business. So now there were drug dealers, cops, and some former Panther comrades who were hunting for us, all of whom definitely would prefer us dead rather than alive.

When you woke up in the morning as a Panther you had the thought that this might be the day that you went to prison or got killed. When you woke up in the morning as a soldier of the Black Liberation Army you had the thought that this was definitely the day that you would die. You were moving too fast, always armed, always in danger of instant confrontation that could wind up with bullets flying.

More opportunities came up for me to get away. I could have gone down south and lived on somebody's farm, slipped back across the border to Canada for another try at Europe and Africa, or made my way to Cuba. I turned all these offers down, justifying my decision by saying that someone had to stay to help build the underground resistance movement. It was the only way to make up for my mistakes and personal failures: not spotting Yedwa as a pig, not getting more of the Panther 21 out on bail, letting Afeni and Joan walk back into prison, going into hiding and abandoning all the young Harlem and Bronx Panthers who looked to me for leadership. No,

I was going to build the resistance or die trying. When the Panther 21 was convicted I would lead the charge of the resistance in storming the prisons to free them.

I was hiding out in a tiny studio apartment in Washington Heights when the news of the Panther 21 verdict came over the small kitchen radio. It was now May 1971. I had been hiding out for two months. Summation and closing arguments in the Panther 21 trial had been going on for the last several weeks. In his instructional charge to the jury, Judge John Murtagh dismissed all of the gun charges. During the long trial there had been much talk about guns, self-defense, and the constitutional right to bear arms. Judge Murtagh said that he wanted to clear away the gun rhetoric so that the jury could focus on the main conspiracy charges. Judge Murtagh's instructions alone took two days. The trial had lasted eight months. To everyone's surprise the jury returned with a verdict in three hours. Deliberations in such big cases usually took days or weeks, so not much deliberation probably meant the jurors' minds had already been made up. I imagined that Afeni, Joan, and the Panthers tried to stand as erect and strong as possible as they were brought into court from their holding cells. The nooses had been fitted tightly around their necks, and the legal lynching was about to be complete.

Clarence Fox, the black jury foreman, read the verdict with a slight West Indian lilt to his voice. It made his pronouncements seem even more surreal and poetic. "Not guilty," he answered when asked about the first count of the indictment. "Not guilty," he repeated dozens of times, as the jury acquitted the Panthers on every single count of the indictment. Gasps of disbelief mingled with tears of joy and cheers of freedom as the two-and-a-half-year nightmare came to an end. Afeni, Lumumba, Joan, Shaba, and the rest of the Panther 21 walked free.

The prosecutors and our lawyers rushed to the jury. The lawyers shook the jurors' hands and thanked them; the prosecutors wanted to know what happened. Mr. Fox and the other jurors explained to the lawyers and the press that they had been convinced that the Panther 21 had been arrested because of their political beliefs, and while they may have been engaged in some illegal activities, there was no proof of a conspiracy to launch guerrilla warfare in New York City. Mr. Fox went on to explain that once the judge dismissed the illegal gun charges, there was nothing to establish a conviction of the Panther 21. So the Panthers did receive justice. Not from the judges and the police system that indicted us, but from twelve people who listened to the arguments and the soul-felt speeches given by the lawyers along with Cet and Afeni.

An eight-months pregnant Afeni had given her summation to the jury, convinced that her son, Tupac Shakur, would be born in prison. "Forgive me if I stray from legal jargon, for I am not a lawyer. I have chosen to defend myself against the advice of cocounsel, the court, friends, and as a matter of fact, against my own intellect. I do it now, as I have in the past, because I know better than any lawyer in America that Afeni Shakur is not guilty of the charges before you. Here I am, scared, shaking, nervous, but full of the knowledge that I cannot beg you for pity. There is no need for that. I am tired. I am sick of this. He [the prosecutor] has not proven any of the charges against me. Why hasn't he proven them? Because he just couldn't. Because there was nothing to prove. So then why are we here? Why are any of us here? I don't know. But I would appreciate it if you would end this nightmare, because I am tired of it. There is no logical reason for us to have gone through the last two years as we have. To be threatened with imprisonment because somebody somewhere is watching and waiting to justify his being a spy. So do what you have to do. Let history record you as a jury who would not kneel to the outrageous bidding of the state. All we ask of you is that you judge us fairly. Please judge us according to the way you want to be judged. That's all I have to say."

"This is the people's victory," I declared as I joyfully danced around the little kitchen in that safe house in the Bronx. I pumped my fists and threw karate kicks in the air when I heard the news, knowing that the credit for this outcome went to the jurors. I imagined the joy the members of the 21 felt walking from the courthouse with their freedom. I wished I could go downtown to join them, but I was still a fugitive. My case had been severed from theirs, so their not guilty verdict didn't apply to me. Plus I had missed a court appearance date and the judge issued a bail-jumping warrant for my arrest. Dhoruba was acquitted in absentia. Later we talked about surrendering ourselves for the bail-jumping charges, which carried five years, but felt we would be set up and murdered by the guards in prison, so we decided we wanted to remain underground.

14

Rite of Passage

A few months earlier, before I went underground, I was walking alone near Washington Square Park in Greenwich Village. I had just given a talk to an organization known as the Committee of Returned Volunteers. These were men and women who had served in the Peace Corps and still met to discuss and be involved in various social causes. The issue of reasonable bail and fair trials for the Panthers was something that they felt they could support.

For whatever reason, I was rolling alone that night. Usually

I was escorted by one or two young Panthers from the Harlem office. That evening I sat on a park bench and watched the gay, straight, and lesbian lovers; the hippies, activists, and dog walkers; the children on roller skates, musicians, magicians, and holy people. I felt the same way I did when I was sitting on Noonie's steps looking at the kids play in my old neighborhood. What if I just stayed here? I thought. Became a blippy (black hippie) who smoked weed, played bongos, lived between Washington Square Park and a commune in Vermont. After an hour or so I left the park and passed a church on Washington Square. The glass-cased announcement board outside the church listed the times for Sunday school and Sunday service. Beneath that was a sign: 36 BLACK PANTHERS–12 POLICE OFFICERS KILLED. This blew my mind. That church members were keeping track of how many Panthers and how many police had died in various battles. That they would care, that they had a perspective that included life lost on both sides amazed me. There was no judgment here, just a tally of human life lost in a battle for change.

A few weeks later I was walking through Harlem with Cet, who had just gotten out of prison on bail and was still awaiting trial. It was nighttime and we were on the corner near the housing projects where Cet grew up. He was known in the neighborhood as Mike Tabor, the All-City basketball star. Cet pointed out a basketball court where some of the greatest games in Harlem had been played and a store that he robbed when he was a heroin addict feeding a hundred-dollar-a-day habit. A childhood friend of Cet's, David, walked up to us. David and Cet crushed each other with a bear hug and grinned from ear to ear. "Mike, everybody in the neighborhood is pulling for you, man. We've all followed the Panther 21 case. It's some bullshit the way they've been trying to frame you brothas and sistas up."

Then the corner became theater as they laughed, mimed, and reenacted adventures from their youth. Cet was catching his breath from a hard laugh when he asked David what he was up to now. David looked at the ground and gave a embarrassed shrug. "I'm a pig," he said. "I joined the force two years ago."

I braced myself in preparation for the verbal, if not physical, ass whipping about to befall David. Cet was one of our most eloquent and powerful spokesmen, and I had seen him tear apart cops, capitalists, and politicians with biting, pointed lines. Instead Cet asked David what his job on the force was.

"Traffic, mainly. Sometimes community patrol. The other guys on the job actually get mad at me because I spend so much time talking to these kids out here about staying out of trouble."

"Then you're a police officer, not a pig," Cet replied. "As long as you remember that you're out here to protect the people as opposed to these capitalist swine, you'll be all right."

In that moment I realized that we had to speak to everyone's humanity. People could choose to be progressive and human, no matter what their job was. A cop wasn't automatically a pig just because he wore a badge. And a Panther wasn't automatically a revolutionary and a servant of the people because he put on a beret. But there was no time to check for humanity as we moved about the city as fugitives. On that day we still had arrest warrants and bounties on our heads, and we had no intention of returning to prison. Like so many before us, from all sides of the political spectrum, victory or death was the mantra.

In early June 1971 a group of us led a raid on an after-hours club in the Bronx, housed in an old two-story warehouse on a dark street. Brother Brick (who had participated in previous drug-den raids), Dhoruba, a stickup artist named Gus, and I left our car and approached the club carrying pistols and automatic weapons. We overpowered the guard at the door and took the long staircase that led from the entrance to the second floor.

Gus had told us there was a side room where dealers shot dice and exchanged large amounts of money and drugs. About thirty people were partying in the main area of the club. We fired a machine-gun burst into the ceiling when one of the club security guards tried to reach for a gun. We herded everyone into a corner and scooped up the drugs and money. Brother Brick, who was the point man, checked the streets from a window as we were about to leave. "There are a million pigs outside," he reported.

We checked other windows and saw police cars and cops with shotguns and rifles taking up positions around the building. A junkie standing across the street had seen us entering the building with guns and flagged down a cop car. I flipped over a pool table and took aim at the door. I believed for sure that the cops would batter down the door and that we would all die in a hail of bullets. Brother Brick took up a firing position near the bar. Dhoruba grabbed me by the arm. "If we start firing in here the pigs are gonna shoot all these people, not just us," he said. I knew Dhoruba was right. No matter that there were heroin dealers there. A lot of people, innocent people who had just come to the club to party, would be slaughtered in the cross fire. We told everyone to leave the club and then stepped out into the night.

I held a .45-caliber handgun behind my back as I pushed the door open. Dhoruba grabbed the gun from me just before I stepped into the street. He saved my life. The moment the door swung open a police spotlight blinded me. Through my squinted eyes I could see numerous police rifles and pistols pointed at me. Had I stepped out of the club with that .45, I would have been riddled with bullets and dead before I hit the ground.

Cops grabbed me and handcuffed me. "That's one of the

dudes who robbed us," a dealer shouted from behind the police barricade. "They got machine guns."

The cops dragged me into an alley and began slapping and
punching me. "What are you doing with that machine gun?"
they asked. "You like shooting cops?" No answer, just contempt in my eyes, which fueled the cops' rage.

They began bouncing my face off the brick wall like it was
a basketball. One cop pulled his pistol. "There ain't gonna be
no fucking trial for you," he said. He pointed the pistol at my
chest.

Something inside me snapped. I could hear it and physi-
cally feel it, like a highway flare being snapped open in my
bowels. I leaped toward the cop, screaming. "Go ahead and
pull the trigger, motherfucker. Shoot me. My life don't mean
shit anyway." Two other cops pulled hard on my handcuffs
and arms to restrain me. I meant every word. If I was going
to die in an alley, it wasn't going to be begging or running.
The cop with the pistol lowered his gun and looked at me like
I was crazy.

People from the club began peeking in the alley. The cops
told them to back up and dragged me to a squad car. They
threw me in the backseat and stomped my testicles before
slamming the door. The squad car raced to the precinct where
cops took me into the building and stood me before the desk
sergeant to be booked. "Armed robbery and weapons possession, Sarge," a cop declared. They took me to the main floor

of the precinct where a gauntlet of cops stood in a double row from the first floor up the staircase to the second floor. I saw a sea of blue, blackjacks, nightsticks, and fists waiting for me. I stiffened and dug my feet into the ground. "Do you have an elevator?" I asked in a burst of gallows humor.

"Get the fuck up the stairs," said the cop who had pulled his pistol on me, as he shoved me into the gauntlet. I put my head down as the cops pounded me. When I slipped, they used knees and kicks to get me back on my feet. They used my handcuffs to finish dragging me up the stairs. They unhand-cuffed me just long enough to finger print and photograph me. Then the beatings started again, right in the squad room, in a corner near a window. I lost consciousness only to be slapped awake again.

The cops rehandcuffed me so that my hands were now in front of me, then used a second pair of handcuffs to cuff me to an overhead radiator pipe. A dozen or so handcuffs fastened together were used like a medieval mace to beat me across the back and ribs. I cursed, spat blood, and tried to kick my attackers. No use. They held my legs and punched me in my stomach, knocking the wind out of me. I could see Dhoruba, Brick, and Gus being beaten in different parts of the squad room. They unhandcuffed me from the radiator and threw me into a cell. My left eye was swollen shut, my lips were puffy and bloody, and my ribs were cracked. I crawled in a corner and tried to find the position that hurt the least.

Time passed, one hour, maybe two. It was hard to tell. Cops massed in front of my holding cell: lieutenants, a captain, older white men in suits. I felt like an attraction at a zoo, a broken monkey in a filthy cage. Cops entered. I was given a hamburger, a cup of tea, and some paper towels. "Clean yourself up," a cop ordered. I went to the sink and used wetted paper towels to dab the dried blood off my face. My mouth was almost swollen shut, so I had to tear the burger into tiny pieces, dip it into the tea, and then shove it into my mouth. I knew I had to keep up my strength. My Panther training had taught me that torture comes in cycles. First, you're interrogated, then tortured, then given a little rest before the next round begins; each cycle worse than before, and so on, until you break.

As we were being punched, stomped, and whipped, the cops were processing our fingerprints. It took hours, often days, to match fingerprints in those days before computers. Even priority cases had to be transmitted via teletype, then matched with a physical file search against police and FBI records. Sooner or later the cops would realize that Dhoruba and I were fugitive Panther leaders from the New York 21. I was sure that the beatings would intensify after that. Detectives took me into an office with desk chairs and a file cabinet. I was handcuffed and shackled to a chair. I wriggled my hands and steeled myself for round two of torture. Rubber hoses, broken fingers, cigarette burns to my genitals—I knew what might come, having heard the stories from other prisoners on Rikers and from Panthers who had been beaten.

The door opened and Yedwa entered. He wore a sport shirt, jeans, sneakers, and a gold detective shield dangling from his neck. Another flare went off in my stomach. The demon clawed at my back. The feelings of anxiety, heartbreak, anger, and betrayal exploded like fireworks. "Power to the people, Jamal," he said as if the last two years of treachery and suffering had not happened.

"What's happening, Ralph?" I asked, spitting his slave name at him like an insult.

He moved close to me, taking in my wounds and bruises. "You look pretty messed up," he said with a tinge of compassion.

"You know how it goes. Your pig buddies have been torturing me for the last few hours," I said matter-of-factly, rejecting all compassion.

Yedwa began bouncing on his feet like a boxer in the corner of the ring. "I know you hate me, Jamal. And I know they're gonna give you a lot of time. You're gonna go upstate and get in top shape so that when you come out you can hunt me down and kill me. But that's okay, cuz I'm gonna be training too and I'll be ready."

I suddenly realized that I had spent the last two years recklessly chasing this moment, the chance to again see the brother-mentor-father who so completely violated my trust and my faith. I bounced my chair around so I could look at him with the eye that wasn't swollen shut. "You're probably right that I'm going to get a lot of time," I said, taking my time with each word. "And you're definitely right that I'm going to be thinking about a lot of shit. But I'm not going to waste a single solitary second thinking about you." Then I bounced my chair to turn away from him. He no longer deserved my gaze or my attention. He stood silently for a long moment, then left. The demon detached from my back and went out the door with him. I felt calm, like the ocean after a violent storm, and right then, though battered and chained, the boy became a man.

15

Posttraumatic Stress Blues

*E*l nombre de tu padre verdadero es Alipio Zorilla,"* Alita, my maternal grandmother, somberly told me. *"Fue un revolucionario que luchó junto con Fidel Castro y Che Guevara."* Your real father's name is Alipio Zorilla. He was a revolutionary who fought alongside of Fidel Castro and Che Guevara. The revelation that floated melodically through the air with my grandmother's Spanish traveled like an electric current from my ears to my gut and my brain.

By then I was twenty-nine years old, wearing an orange

jumpsuit in a federal prison visiting room. While I had escaped prosecution as part of the Panther 21 government conspiracy, it was, somewhat ironically, my efforts as a part of the team working to rid Harlem of the insidious drug trade that ultimately landed me in prison for the first time. Out at age twenty-one, I was now back in prison, again because of acting on my political beliefs. Alita and her sister Elena had come to visit. My sister, Elba, was also there. Aunt Elena still lived in Cuba and, after years of trying, finally received a visa to visit New York. How she got into a federal prison with a Cuban passport was beyond my comprehension. Or maybe the officials wanted to see what connection I had to Cuba. Certainly the reasoning was more complex than I or the guards, who were probably electronically monitoring the conversation, could imagine. "You're such a sweet boy, *mi hijo,*" Aunt Elena said, pinching my cheeks. "You don't belong in prison. It's your father. You have his blood, and he's crazy. He's a tall, handsome man. *Muy inteligente.* But he's crazy. He fought in the mountains with Fidel, and he comes to the towns to give big speeches. Then he disappears for a few days and pow, *una bomba,* a big explosion in that town. And then your father reappears."

"Grandma, Auntie," I stammered in my jailhouse-acquired, self-taught Spanish. "Thank you so much for finally telling me who my real father is. I've wanted to know for a long time, but I'm not sure if my politics is a genetic condition." The sweet old ladies continued to pinch my cheeks and share stories about Cuba and my mother.

They reminisced about the house in Santa Clara, Cuba, which had a pool and a servant. They reminisced about my grandfather Alfredo, originally from the island of Dominica, who immigrated to Cuba and became a prosperous engineer. My uncle Ruben, Gladys's younger brother, would tell stories of taking his friends for food and milkshakes after school at a fancy hotel in Santa Clara, then telling the waiter to "put it on my father's tab." Gladys learned French from a tutor, had a debutante ball when she was a teenager, and drove her friends around in a convertible she received as a high school graduation present. She was a straight-A student and an amazing poet who would recite original and classic Spanish poems with a passion that made listeners cry. My uncle said that traffic stopped and men turned their heads when Gladys walked down the street. Instead of being jealous, girls flocked around her, drawn to her vibrant personality and generous spirit.

Gladys went to Havana where she flourished as a premed student. She met Alipio in graduate school and fell in love. Alipio was already a member of the Communist Party and was a fiery and charismatic organizer at the university. Gladys was home in Santa Clara on semester break when she realized she was pregnant. Before she could tell Alipio that she was carrying his child, she found out that he gotten his distant cousin pregnant and announced that he would do the right thing and marry her. Gladys tearfully confessed the love affair and pregnancy to Alita. She asked to be taken to the family doctor to get rid of the baby. Alita felt Gladys's stomach and told her that she was too far along to have an abortion, and thus Gladys was sent to New York, where I was born.

Gladys placed me in "temporary care" while she learned English, earned a second bachelor's and a master's degree from Brooklyn College in biology, and got a job in the hospital as a lab technician. A few years later she married my stepfather, Luis, a former boxer and laborer, and gave birth to my younger sister and brother, Elba and Luis Jr. The family lived in a small apartment in Brooklyn while Gladys and Luis saved money for a house. She got her pharmacist's license and was a step closer to the dream. She died in childbirth, just days after putting a down payment on a house in Brooklyn.

Alipio and Gladys wrote letters to each other even after she moved to New York and was married. Luis would tear the letters up in a jealous rage and demand that Gladys not write him. Soon after, Alipio disappeared in the mountains of Cuba to fight the revolution. My grandmother and aunt told me that Alipio eventually became a general in the Cuban military, a minister of the interior, and Cuba's ambassador to Tanzania.

After their visit, I went back to my cell and wrote my father a long, impassioned letter and sent it via my auntie, who gave it to her daughter, a mathematics professor at the University of Havana and a friend of Alipio's. My letter explained that

I was in prison for my Black Panther beliefs and activities, suggesting that perhaps he had indeed passed on the DNA of agitation, rebellion, and revolution. I heard a few weeks later that the letter had reached him, but I never received a reply. Maybe he was in too delicate a situation or embroiled in some Cuban political intrigue that would compromise him if people became aware that he had a bastard American son. Yet it was hard for me to imagine having a son somewhere out there in the world and not trying to find him.

The twelve years that passed from the night I sat in chains talking to Yedwa to where I was now, sitting in a Leavenworth cell, were intense. I spent the rest of my teenage years in various state prisons for the robbery charges. Not long after I began my sentence, the Attica rebellion happened in upstate New York. The men took control of the prison protesting the guards' brutality, as well as the food and living conditions, and they demanded access to legal and social services. What made the rebellion powerful was the solidarity among the prisoners. Black, white, red, brown, and yellow prisoners stood together in their demands. There was a Marxist revolutionary undertone in the writing and statements of the prisoners. Attorney William Kunstler and Panther founder Bobby Seale were part of the negotiating team, working on behalf of the prisoners.

At first the guards in our prison let us watch the news coverage of Attica on the rec room TV. By the second day the TV was gone. By the third day we were on lockdown, as was every other prison throughout the country. New York governor Nelson Rockefeller broke off the negotiations with the Attica prisoners and ordered an army of state troopers to retake the prison. The troopers fired tear gas and sprayed bullets nonstop for several minutes. When the shooting stopped, thirty-nine people lay dead in the prison yard, ten of them guards and civilian employees. It was first reported that the guards who were being held hostage were executed by the prisoners. The truth was that they died from the same indiscriminate gunfire that killed the prisoners.

I knew some of the guys who died in Attica. We had been on Rikers Island and at the Elmira Reception Center together. I looked at the newspaper pictures of the aftermath of the rebellion and knew that it could easily have been me lying in the blood and mud of Attica prison. It was one of the places the prison officials considered sending me to when I began my sentence.

Two weeks before the rebellion a prison leader named George Jackson was shot to death by guards in California's San Quentin prison. The guards claimed that he had smuggled in a gun and was trying to escape. Most people believed that George was murdered and the gun was planted near his body after the fact. George Jackson had been sentenced to seventy years for a gas station robbery when he was seventeen years old. To the system he was another poor black kid who couldn't afford a lawyer. Like Malcolm X, George educated himself and became a brilliant jailhouse scholar and lawyer. He was a self-proclaimed Marxist revolutionary, and he helped organize chapters of the Black Panther Party throughout the California prison system. He became a best-selling author with his books *Soledad Brother* and *Blood in My Eye*. George's great offense against the system wasn't the petty robbery but his charismatic presence and his ability to create truces and organize warring racial prison gangs.

George Jackson's murder and the Attica rebellion created a revolutionary spirit among prisoners around the country. Prison newspapers were founded and prisoners created political cadres and solidarity movements. At Leavenworth I organized, agitated, and spent a fair amount time "in the hole" as a result of confrontations with the guards. When they had too much of me in one place, I would be transferred to another facility and the cycle would start again. I earned a high school equivalency diploma and petitioned to be transferred to a prison that offered college courses. Since this was the one thing I really wanted, the officials took great pleasure in denying my request.

I was released from prison on my twenty-first birthday. This was pure coincidence and not a birthday gift from the prison authorities. I returned to a Harlem that felt and looked like a scorched battlefield. Drugs had become a pandemic. Some blocks resembled the aftermath of bombing raids. I walked down streets I had traveled as a confident young Panther, now feeling like we had lost the war, which meant that my young comrades had died in vain. No one talked much about the Panthers anymore. When people found out I was a former Panther who served time, they usually went the other way. There was fear in the air. So many Panthers and Panther sympathizers had been killed, locked up, or had their lives ruined by detectives and FBI agents who would show up to get them fired from jobs, evicted from homes, and expelled from school.

I took classes at Brooklyn College, worked various jobs, and used a student loan to buy a gypsy cab. I taught karate classes in Harlem, the Lower East Side, and Brooklyn. My friends Imara "Green Eyes" Diaz, Taiwan Delain, and I opened a small karate dojo in Williamsburg, Brooklyn. We hung pictures of Che Guevara, Don Pedro Albizu Compos (a Puerto Rican nationalist leader), and Malcolm X next to those of the Asian martial arts masters. The black and Latino kids who were our students learned about their history and progressive movements as they were learning punches, kicks, flips, and rolls. We charged ten dollars a month for unlimited lessons and five dollars for uniforms. Even though the prices were cheap and we had plenty of students, we were always in the red. The kids were too poor to pay the dues. I would drive twelve-hour shifts in my gypsy cab to pay the dojo rent and the rent on my tiny one-bedroom apartment, but I loved what we were doing. The movie *Enter the Dragon* had been tops at the box office a year earlier, and every kid in the neighborhood wanted to be Bruce Lee. Maybe the oppressor had destroyed the Black Panther Party and crushed the movement, I thought, but my young dojo warriors would be the next generation of revolutionaries.

Our top young student was an eleven-year-old Puerto Rican boy named Angel. He was cute and curly-haired, with soft brown eyes, destined to be impossibly handsome as he grew into manhood. Angel was the first to show up every day and the last to leave at night. I would sit with him in our little office/lounge in the back of the dojo to make sure he did his homework. In the mode of life in the Chinese Buddhist temples, Angel would help me sweep, mop, wash windows, and maintain the dojo. This way he earned his lessons and would feel good about the two or three dollars I would slip in his pocket. Angel had brilliant martial arts technique and high flashy kicks. He would imitate the way I sparred and did forms. When we did karate demonstrations at community centers and tournaments, the crowd would get a kick out of seeing Angel and me performing as large and small versions of each other.

We would share a pizza, a hot dog, or a chicken patty, and I would ask Angel what he wanted to be when he grew up. His answer was to ask me, "What do you want to be?" to which I would say, "I don't know. I think I'll finish college and be a teacher or a social worker."

Angel would smile and say, "Then I want to be a teacher or a social worker."

I would say, "Angel, what kind of car do you want to drive?" and he would say, "I don't know. What kind of car do you want?"

I would answer, "I don't know, maybe a Camaro or a Jaguar." His eyes would sparkle and he would say, "Then I want a Camaro or a Jaguar." We'd finish our lunch and then talk about Bruce Lee, baseball, and traveling to Japan and China to meet the great martial arts masters.

Angel earned his black belt right after he turned thirteen. It was summer, just before the Fourth of July. The temperature was hot and the streets were filled with people hanging out and dancing to the music coming from the open tenement windows and record players blasting Latin and soul music. Kids were starting to set off firecrackers as a lead-up to the holiday. The sidewalk firework salesmen were just letting go of a few packs of firecrackers as a tease, timing their big business for a day or two before the Fourth.

Angel was buying soda in a bodega with some friends when he heard a series of pops right outside the grocery store door. "Firecrackers!" he shouted happily as he pulled out a dollar and ran outside to see if he could buy a pack or two. The firecracker pops were actually rival drug dealers shooting it out on the street in front of the bodega, and when Angel stepped out on the street he was shot between the eyes.

"What do you want to be, Angel?"—our conversations haunted me for months after his death.

"What do you want to be?" he answered, eyes sparkling, full of hope. "Whatever you want to be, that's what I want to be."

Angel's murder rocked me to the core. The demon of death that I thought I had purged was once again riding my back. I drifted away from teaching karate and from the counseling jobs I had at a drug center and a youth program. Who was I to teach or counsel anybody?

The gypsy cab still paid the bills. In fact, I saved enough money to buy another gypsy cab, which I leased out. I started numbing out using weed, alcohol, and sometimes coke to ease the pain. I went into a kind of self-imposed exile. I didn't want to think or talk about the Panther movement. Didn't want to remember or deal with the battles and the open wounds that were still searing my memories and ravaging my dreams. I hung out with an eclectic group that included street people, artists, and folks from the night life. I hustled just enough to support my habit. My "deals and introductions" were among my small circle of friends. We fancied ourselves outlaws, sharing contempt for the system and the "square life." Even so, I would have bouts of depression and guilt, feeling that I had fallen victim to some of the habits and behavior that I fought against as a young Panther.

Politics wasn't completely gone from the mix. I had some of my best discussions about human rights, social issues, and progressive politics in the backs of bars and in after-hours joints with hustlers, hookers, and thieves.

I was still wild and reckless, ready to roll with any friend who had a problem or beef on the street. My demon continued to whisper through my subconscious. I didn't die in a blaze of glory during the revolution; maybe I could still have a samurai-like warrior's death on the street.

That chance would come on a summer night in 1980. I was cooling out listening to jazz in my Greenwich Village apartment. It was a neat little hideaway—a small one-bedroom garden apartment with a fireplace. It had two exits, one through the courtyard and another through the main building, perfect for a posttraumatic-stress suffering former Panther who was ready to spring into any kind of action. My phone rang with the proper code. Two rings. Hang up. Call back. (This is how it worked before the days of caller ID and cell phones.) "Yeah," I answered, as flat and cold as possible. I didn't like phones. I did time with too many people who, like me, listened to hours of wiretaps and dumb conversations during their trials.

"It's Jake," came the frantic teenage voice through the receiver. "I just got into some shit with some crazy dude in the bar."

"Okay. Be cool," I said, not wanting to hear any details over the phone. "I'll meet you on the corner." I threw on a shirt and headed out to meet Jake on the corner of Hudson and Perry close to my apartment.

Jake was an eighteen-year-old white kid from the Midwest whose mom was part of our night-life circle of friends. He and I bonded over Bruce Lee movies, and I had been giving him karate lessons in the park for about six months. When I saw Jake, his shirt was covered with blood.

"What happened, man?" I asked as I inspected his face and arms for cuts.

"It's not my blood. It's this bouncer named Nelson. We had some words about me getting off the pool table and he shoved me. I pushed him back and he rushed me. I popped him with a backhand you showed me and cracked his nose."

I told Jake to come back to my pad so he could clean up. He had lost his wallet in the scuffle and wanted to go back to the bar and look for it.

Even though this was the West Village, generally a safe place, this was a shady bar, and I had warned Jake about hanging out there, but he liked the pool table—plus they let him drink without checking ID. We checked around the bar for his wallet with no luck. As we were walking up Greenwich Street, Nelson, the muscular thirty-year-old bouncer, rode up on a bike. "That's the guy," Jake whispered.

Nelson got off his bike, leaned it against a telephone post, and said calmly, "Oh, there you go. I been looking for you." He was about twenty feet away. Jake walked over to talk to him. I lay back, not wanting the bouncer to feel that I was there to pose a threat, especially since they were about to talk it out.

The bouncer reached into his crotch and withdrew a small pistol. I recognized it as a .25, maybe .32, caliber. The action seemed disconnected from his mellow demeanor. I couldn't believe he was pulling out a gun. So I froze, watching. Unbelieving. He raised the gun and pointed it at Jake. "Don't shoot me, man," Jake pleaded. His frightened voice startled me out of my daze.

"Jake, run," I yelled in a commanding tone. The bouncer pulled the trigger twice as Jake rushed past him. I looked around for a weapon. Thank God for dirty New York City streets. There was a half-empty beer bottle in the gutter. I swooped it up and hurtled it at the bouncer, cracking him in the back of the head. He spun around and fired at me. I ducked and rolled into the street.

I looked over my shoulder as I was sprinting away and saw Jake limping badly. The bouncer was running behind him, firing. My legs wanted to keep running to safety. My gut knew that Jake was a dead man if I didn't do something. I leaped over the hood of a parked car and got myself between Jake and the bouncer.

"You gotta run, man," I urged.

"I can't," Jake answered in pain. "My leg."

"Bullshit," I said. "We're running tonight."

I grabbed the back of his belt with one hand and his shirt collar with the other and dragged him along with me. We ran around and ducked between parked cars as the bouncer kept firing. How many damn bullets does that thing have? I thought as the bullets whizzed by. Time does slow in the midst of high intensity stress. I had experienced it before on different occasions when bullets from drug dealers and cops flew by my head, and the seconds that night felt like long, drawn-out minutes. Finally the gun clicked empty and the bouncer hopped on his bike and raced off.

I threw Jake's arm around my shoulder and headed toward the nearest precinct, which was two blocks away. Cops were running up the street toward the sound of the gunfire. The police captain reached us first. He saw that Jake was wounded. "What happened?" he asked.

"A guy tried to rob us. He shot my friend." The captain instructed a cop to take us into the precinct. Good move, I thought.

Ambulances were notoriously slow in answering sidewalk calls in New York, but a gunshot call from a precinct should make them materialize instantly. I was wrong. Jake sat on the bench bleeding, with the color draining from his face. He threw up and went into shock. Several white cops stood around, just looking. I asked for paper towels so I could clean Jake up and put pressure on his wounds.

When I lifted his shirt, I saw two bullet wounds going into his back. This made me nervous. I had seen people shot in the torso who seemed fine but then died a few hours later from the internal damage. I rushed over to the desk sergeant. "Can

you call the ambulance again, please? He's going into shock."
That's when I felt a sharp pain in my arm and noticed a bullet
wound near my elbow.

The ambulance finally came and took us to St. Vincent's
Hospital. The doctors found that Jake had been shot three
times but had sustained no major damage. My bullet chipped
a bone and hurt like hell, but my arm would be okay. Jake and
I were moved to a small ward.

The hospital staff didn't know what to make of the parade
of visitors who came by while I was there. They included
black, white, Latino, Middle Eastern, hardened ex-cons, radical lawyers, young Wall Street guys, overly dramatic actors,
and a black and white six-foot-four drag queen duo named
Eileen and Bianca. I had walked into an acting class on a
whim a few months earlier, and I loved it. I became immersed
in the improv, classical, and technique training. The teachers
invited me to become part of the Actors Playhouse Ensemble,
and I acted in several of its off-Broadway productions.

Several months after the shooting, I was subpoenaed to
testify at the bouncer's trial. I had given the police little information about the shooting, with the intention of solving the
problem in my own way. Jake identified the bouncer, which
resulted in his arrest for attempted murder. I testified honestly
that I didn't remember much about the person who shot me.
The bouncer was acquitted of the charges and Jake moved
back to the Midwest.

A few weeks later I saw the bouncer on the street. He called me over and apologized for shooting me. Our respective street networks had given the bouncer and me a lot of information about each other. I knew that he was connected to the Columbian and Italian mobs. He knew I was a former Panther. We had both served time and knew the rules of prison and the street. He also knew that I had honored the "no snitch" code. "Whatever you want to make things right—ten grand, cocaine, whatever—you got," the bouncer said with a sneer, a mixture of apology and arrogance. "But that kid was disrespectful in the bar and a snitch in the courtroom. He's still going to get his."

I looked at the bouncer, who was calm yet deadly intent, the way he was when he shot us on Greenwich Street. "Here's what I want to make things right. I want you to forget about your beef with this kid the way I'm gonna forget about my beef with you." My posture told him that this would be the deal or this would be war. Finally the bouncer shook my hand, and the beef was squashed. The code of the street, the honor and word of the street soldier.

Several years passed and I continued teaching karate, acting, and hanging out with friends ranging from artists to outlaws. I also stayed in touch with a number of my Panther comrades, some of whom were fugitives on local and federal charges. My wide range of friends gave me connections to vacant apartments, fake documents, and contacts in different countries. I began helping "movement people" on the run with places to stay, fake IDs, and safe routes out the country. I believed that the government had jailed Panthers on trumped-up charges and was happy to help other former Panthers and young radicals avoid prison. I was willing to help Panthers who had escaped from prison too.

Disco fever had swept the country, and it was now the late 1980s. But Harlem, like other poor communities, was literally crumbling. There were endless blocks that looked like London after a bombing raid. Slumlords had walked away rather than pay taxes. The city took over the properties but did nothing to repair the decay. Poor families still lived in some of these buildings, without heat and with electricity stolen via long extension cords connected to streetlamps. There were community organizers trying to help, but much of the black revolutionary movement had been destroyed or driven "underground" by police raids and the FBI COINTELPRO attacks. Those of us who were still in contact felt like we were part of a "resistance" that needed to survive by any means necessary until the movement could regroup.

One night, in July 1981, a lawyer friend named Harold Briscoe stopped by my apartment in the Village with his dinner date, a stunning woman named Joyce Walker. Joyce was an actress, dancer, and model who had been part of the original Broadway cast of *Hair*. She had also been the first black woman on the cover of *Seventeen* magazine. She graduated from Long Island University with a philosophy degree and had decided to put her artistic career on hold to attend law school. Joyce let me know that Harold was not a real date but a law school mentor. She and I went on a date and fell in love. Within six months we were married and Joyce was pregnant with our first child.

Three months after that the FBI kicked our door in at four in the morning. Agents dragged me from the bedroom while a two-hundred-pound agent sat on Joyce's back and pointed an M16 at her head. "Get off me, I'm pregnant!" I heard her angrily yell. I fought to get to her but was cuffed and dragged from the apartment. I was tried in federal court and convicted of being an accessory after the fact for hiding fugitives who were wanted by the FBI. I was sentenced to twelve and a half years. Joyce sat in the courtroom holding our now one-year-old son Jamal Jr.

16

Leavenworth University

The prison bus pulled up in front of the large structure that resembled the domed Capitol Building in Washington DC. Cell blocks jutted out from the dome, making it look like a giant concrete octopus. A sixty-foot wall with a barbed-wire crown surrounded the complex. Gun towers were placed strategically both inside and outside of the wall. This was Leavenworth Federal Penitentiary, a maximum-security facility that convicts unaffectionately called "the big top."

There were forty of us chained and shackled, hand, waist, and foot. Guards led us off the prison bus and up the long row of steps to the main entrance. On either side was a gauntlet of guards holding M16 military assault rifles, each man with a give-me-an-excuse glint in his eye. Inside the main gates we were greeted by a captain, a redneck ex-Marine in his fifties who appeared to be still fit and combat ready. The captain spoke to us in his southern drawl: "Welcome to Leavenworth Federal Penitentiary. If you convicts are here, then you have worked hard to get here, so let me quickly introduce you to your home for the next few years. Down this corridor to your right is the guard house, commonly known as 'the hole.' You fuck up once, that's your first stop. Down this corridor to your left is the infirmary. You fuck up twice, that's your second stop. Beyond the sixty-foot wall and the gun towers is a patch of land that holds the cow pasture and the prison cemetery. Need I say more?"

With that, we were processed in and led to the cell block that served as the reception center. The average prisoner in Leavenworth was serving fifty years, with many doing life: bank robbery, kidnapping, murder, organized crime, major drug dealers. This is where the elite of the hard core was sent to serve hard time. White-collar criminals got to serve time in one of the minimum-security prison camps that people hear about on the news.

I had been sentenced to twelve and a half years for hiding out people wanted on federal robbery and conspiracy charges. I was now twenty-nine years old, back in prison after eight

years of posttraumatic stress blues. My wild post-Panther ride
had led from the streets, night life, and theater back to revolutionary comrades living underground.

The big yard in Leavenworth had a patchy sports field that
included basketball rims, a handball court, and a weight area.
There was a sweat lodge that had been built when Native
American prisoners won a court battle to allow them to practice their religion. Around the yard, prisoners grouped according to racial backgrounds and gang affiliations. The areas
that they stood in had distinct boundaries and were known as
courtyards or courts. The Aryan Brotherhood, the Mexican
mafia, the Italian mob, and the Black Revolutionary Collective were among the groups controlling territory. No prisoner
stepped into another prisoner's court uninvited. There were
neutral areas of the yard where prisoners mingled for workouts, sports, or business, which was mainly gambling, loan-
sharking, and drugs. Violation of the court rules or of the
convict code could easily lead to death. The sentence for killing another convict was about ten years. What's that on top
of fifty or a hundred years, or even a life sentence? The rules
were reinforced by a prison culture that exploits weakness.

The convict code:

1. Don't snitch on another convict or anyone.
2. Don't steal from another convict.
3. Do your own time.

The same way there are tens of thousands of U.S. laws meant to enforce the Ten Commandments, there are dozens of ways one could violate the convict code and get killed. Stealing from another convict could be interpreted as grabbing the last piece of meat in the chow line or taking another convict's seat in the auditorium on movie night. Leavenworth had Christians, Jews, Muslims, Buddhists, Marxists, nationalists, anarchists, Neo-Nazis, Yogis, and occultists, but the convict code superseded all beliefs and ideologies. A Christian snitch would catch a knife just as quickly as an atheist.

During orientation, the guards instructed us to look for a movement sheet that was posted each day at the front of the cell block. The sheet was a printout with prisoners' names, numbers, and any special moves that were happening for them on that day. Regular routines such as work assignments, meal times, and so forth were not posted on a daily basis. But parole board hearings, infirmary visits, cell block changes, and release dates were posted. If I were going to the infirmary the listing would be "Joseph, 0337, Infirmary 0900 hours." A prisoner going to the parole board would be listed as "Jones, 3421, Parole Board 1100 hours."

A young prisoner, whom I'll call Johnny Smith, was raped and stabbed to death on the top tier of my cell block the first week I arrived at Leavenworth. He was due to be released in a few weeks, and a group of his homeboys got drunk with him on homemade liquor and held him down. Maybe they thought he wouldn't tell. Maybe they were jealous that he had gotten parole. His body was placed in one of the eight-foot laundry bags used to collect sheets and left in a shower stall. The entire prison was locked down. Our cells were searched and we were made to step outside naked so the guards could check our bodies for scratches or wounds. I thought we would be locked in our cells for days or a week, but the next morning the cell doors opened at 6 a.m. so we could march to breakfast and go to our work assignments. Word was that the guys who killed Johnny had been arrested and thrown in the hole. I stopped at the front of the cell block and looked at the movement sheet as instructed. I saw my name listed for an infirmary visit at 0800 hours. Below me was an entry for the young prisoner who had been killed. "Smith, Johnny, 78127, Parole by Death."

I stared at the movement sheet frozen, shaken, hardened, baptized in the realization that I was in a place where I might also be "paroled by death."

Don't snitch on another convict. Don't steal from another convict. Do your own time. I set my focus on rule number three—I would do my own time. No organizing. No joining a prison clique. No getting involved with other people's beefs, and especially no gambling, no drugs, no sex, these being three of the main activities that created prison beefs.

One day I sat in the prison yard reading a book, as alone and as minding-my-business as I could be. An older black prisoner named Mr. Cody walked over to me. Suave, savvy, confident, he was a man who on the streets ran a bank robbery ring and gambling joints and in prison continued to "run a few things."

"Say, youngblood, I hear you was down with the Black Panthers and things," said Mr. Cody, asking a question that was really a statement.

"Yes, sir," I answered, looking up from my book.

"I hear you down with a little karate and things," he continued.

"Yes, sir," I answered, not too surprised that my Black Panther and karate rep had followed me to Leavenworth.

"And I hear you was down with some plays and things out there."

"Yeah?" I answered, surprised that anyone in the joint knew about my foray into theater back in the Village.

"Uh-huh," Mr. Cody said stroking his chin. Then he walked away.

I headed back to my cell a little anxious and concerned. Did the fact that I performed in a few plays violate the convict code? Would the other prisoners perceive me as soft and come at me in the shower or when the lights went down on movie night in the auditorium? The next day I finished my work assignment sweeping and mopping the library and gym. I returned to my reading spot in the big yard. Suddenly there was an eclipse. I looked up expecting to see the moon blocking the sun and instead saw Mr. Cody standing with two massive black prisoners. They looked like NFL linebackers but were marked with knife scars and bullet wounds, like death had struck them. In fact, those were their names: Death and Struck. "Hey, youngblood, about them plays," Mr. Cody said with a half smile.

This is it, I thought, the convict code is about to punish me for my theater days. "Yeah," I said as I got to my feet.

"I want you to pull together a little show for Black History Month. I done worked it out with the warden."

With that Mr. Cody, Death, and Struck were gone, and like it or not, I had my assignment.

I went to the prison library and found copies of only two plays—*Romeo and Juliet,* which was definitely out of the question, and *A Raisin in the Sun* by Lorraine Hansberry. I showed the play to Mr. Cody in the mess hall that night. "I only found one black play and it has women in it," I explained.

"That's okay, youngblood," he said, smiling. "Just look around the mess hall and pick out two or three you want in the play, and we'll put dresses on them." I couldn't tell if he was joking about the dresses, but he wouldn't be deterred from me putting on some kind of Black History Month show.

I went back to my cell, grabbed a pad and pencil, and began writing a play. I called it *Parole by Death.* The setting: Death Row—five men struggling with the criminal misjustice system and their conscience, days before there is to be a lottery to decide which one of them will die.

In addition to being an actress, my wife, Joyce, was a playwright whose work had been produced by Joseph Papp and Woodie King Jr. She sent me copies of her plays and other scripts so I could understand more about dramatic structure and format. Joyce would send me the plays to study, as would my good friend and attorney Bill Mogulescu. They would make sure the plays came via bookstores or theater companies. Had they come through regular mail, the guards would have simply trashed them.

Mr. Cody secured a rehearsal space in a storage room near the gym. He also provided the cast: Death and Struck, neither of whom had an interest in acting. But Mr. Cody had aspirations of being a producer, and what Mr. Cody wanted, Mr. Cody got. As part of our rehearsals, I developed a technique of teaching acting through improv. I would create a situation that people were familiar with, throw them in the mix, and then deconstruct the scene to show them what acting techniques they had been using without realizing.

"Freeze," I shouted at a heightened moment in a scene between Death and Struck. They were panting and staring each other down like boxers in the ring. "Death, Struck. Wow, that was amazing! I really felt your commitment to your characters and to the scene. Death, you looked at Struck with such intensity when you told him you would stab him fifteen times and eat his liver for a snack. Struck, you were so present when you told Death you were gonna bash in his skull with the mop wringer until his brains oozed out of his ears. Great damn work!"

They continued to stare at each other as I moved from praise to deconstruction. "Now, when an actor gives a long talk or a speech, like I'm doing, that's called a monologue. When two actors are talking back and forth, the way you guys were, that's called dialogue. Say that with me: dialogue."

Death kept staring at Struck and barely moved his lips as he growled. "I wasn't dialogin'! I'm gonna kill this fool for real."

Struck seemed to swell twice his size with anger. "You'll be dead before you can blink, punk-ass son of a bitch."

I jumped between them and grunted as I struggled to push them apart. "Okay, fellas. Let's go back to our centering exercise. This is how we get rid of that negative emotion. Feet together, hands up, and breathe. You're a tree." I raised my arms and spread them as I demonstrated the yogalike posture. "Once again; breathe. You're a tree." Death and Struck looked at me like I was crazy.

At that moment Tito and Raphael, two of the leaders of the Latino crew LaRasa, strolled into the rehearsal space. Tito and Raphael had six or seven murders between them since they'd been in the joint. They had killed people in prison hallways, corridors, and mess halls in plain view of the guards, almost chuckling as the guards handcuffed them afterwards. "Give me the ten years," they would taunt. "You want to take away my driver's license while you're at it?"

Of all the prison crews, LaRasa was the worst to have a beef with. They would pursue a vendetta to the bitter end. A LaRasa member who worked in the plumbing shop would toss a piece of metal out of the window into the big yard. Another member would file the metal against concrete every day for a month, shaping it into an ice pick. He would get a piece of plastic wrap from a LaRasa member who worked in the kitchen, get Vaseline or antibacterial ointment from another member who worked in the infirmary, wrap the ice pick in plastic, lubricate it, then insert it in his anus so he could bring it through the metal detector into the main prison. He would mount it on a piece of wood and use it to take out the vendetta victim in front of everybody in the cell block.

Tito and Raphael sat on a broken workout bench and watched the rehearsal. Death, Struck, and I were in telepathic communication with the same thought: LaRasa has left their court and come to our rehearsal. Who are they here to kill? One of the unwritten statutes of the convict code goes "The main thing is just don't panic." So everyone acted cool. Death and Struck put their arms up and started swaying with me. "Look, Jamal, I'm a tree," Death grunted. "I'm a palm tree." Still looking at Tito and Raphael out of the corner of our eyes, we began rehearsing and improvising one of the scenes from the play.

Tito kept shifting his muscular tattooed frame like something was disturbing him. He silently grew angrier and angrier. A few minutes later he stood up, pointed at me, and grimaced. "Yo, *ese*, let me talk to you a minute." He pulled me into a corner and bored into me with a cobralike stare. I shifted my feet into a neutral karate stance, arms at my side but ready for an attack. Just be cool, Jamal, I coached myself. Talk to him man to man, don't be too timid or aggressive, but if you see him reach around to his asshole for a knife, try to take the whole damn arm and run out the gym for help.

"Yo, *ese*. We know what you're up here doing," Tito said, leaning in close, "because there ain't no secrets in the big top. But I had to come to check it out for myself. I been sitting here watching this shit for about ten minutes and I'm gonna tell you something, *ese*, that guy you're working with, that fucking guy, *ese*, he's not feeling his character."

"Well, Tito, why don't you jump into the scene and try," I said, flabbergasted that he was actually here to critique the acting.

"You ain't said nothing but a thing, *ese*," Tito replied as he took off his bandanna and joined Death and Struck. Turns out that Tito had done plays in high school and showed a lot of promise as an actor even while he was gangbanging. He jumped into the scene and was terrific, not only at acting but at getting Death and Struck to relax too. Rafael also joined the group. That night I rewrote the play to include Latino characters.

A few days later, a white prisoner named Reb, who was a

member of the Aryan Brotherhood, came to rehearsal. Reb
was a fourth-degree black belt in Tae Kwon Do. He and I had
whipped each other's asses on a couple of occasions during
a "friendly workout." It was really a mutual test to see if the
Panther or the Aryan was a better martial artist. Both the
matches were a draw and we headed back to the cell blocks
with lots of bruises and mutual respect, at least when it came
to karate. Reb came to rehearsal to see if the blacks and Lati-
nos were forming an alliance. He left with a role in the play.

That night I rewrote the play again to add a white character.
Over the next few weeks, more prisoners joined the ensemble,
black, white, Latino, Native American. The word "truce" was
never spoken, but it was understood that our creative space
needed to be a safe space where beefs and affiliations were
excluded. In effect, we created our own court. We would im-
provise, rehearse, and argue near the bleachers in the big yard.
"You expect me to say these lines, Jamal? What's my motivation?" I would shake my head and use my pencil to scribble a
new line as we continued to have a theater troupe fight under
the shadow of the gun tower.

The warden and the prison administration were suspicious
and skeptical about our play, especially when we asked permission to build a theater set. We wrote a letter, had a meeting
in the warden's office, and invited him to a rehearsal, which
he refused to attend. It looked like the whole play was in jeop-
ardy until the recreation supervisor, Mr. Rathmore, agreed

to help. Mr. Rathmore was an African American athlete who went to college on a football scholarship. He became a correction officer and was promoted to recreation supervisor, a job that was more about coaching and counseling than lockdowns and beat-downs. Mr. Rathmore agreed to do overtime without pay to supervise our set construction. Even with Mr. Rathmore putting his reputation, if not his job, on the line, the most the warden would agree to was one performance, with one day to build the set and one night to tear it down.

Mr. Rathmore understood the value of education and arts in prison. He let us use the storage room for our play rehearsals. He also set up a music room and used part of his recreation budget to buy used instruments. A few of the prisoners had played on the outside and were pretty good musicians. They approached me about forming a pit band that could be part of the show. That *Parole by Death* was meant to be a heavy drama, not a musical, seemed not to deter them. I went back to my cell and rewrote the play once again so that there was "musical narration" in the beginning, middle, and end. By now the cast had grown to fifteen guys. Plus there were stagehands, lighting and sound techs, and the band. The Black History Month play had transformed into a major, multicultural production.

There was still one other obstacle to deal with, though. Convicts were some of the best hecklers on the planet. I had seen fights break out during prison football and softball games because of the heckling coming from the sidelines. "Ray Charles could catch the ball better than you, you hunch-back, gimp-legged, fraud-ass son of a bitch." Movie night was even worse. The hecklers would crack jokes and hurl insults that were so funny that, had they been able to hear them, the screen actors no doubt would have been reduced to tears.

My actors were some of the baddest dudes in the peniten-tiary. They had robbed banks; killed people; shot it out with FBI agents; and stared down knife blades, gun barrels, and in one case, a tank. But stage fright was kicking their asses. I could see the jitters mounting as we got closer to performance day. Despite my pep talks and relaxation exercises, I could tell that my actors were feeling "some type of way" about getting on stage in front of their convict peers. So I decided to send my cast into battle early. I organized a "heckler's rehearsal," a sneak preview where the best hecklers in the joint could go hard at the cast. The hecklers were good, and they did not dis-appoint. "Oh, so Leon, you think you're an actor now? Why don't you act like you gonna pay me those cigarettes you owe me, punk?" At first the actors would crack up or get mad, but by the end of rehearsal they had learned to ignore the insults, dodge the jokes, and stay in character.

When we opened the curtains a few nights later, the ex-pected jeers and insults came from the packed auditorium, but the actors kept on going. Five minutes into the play, an amazing thing happened. The audience kept shouting out comments, but they were in context with the action on stage. As the play continued, they grew quiet during the tense moments and roared during the funny ones. At the end they stood and gave the actors—their peers, their cell mates, in some cases their enemies—a five-minute standing ovation.

The warden and the guards were convinced that there would be trouble during the play. Captain Foster thought the whole thing was a hoax, a distraction for an escape attempt or a gang war. The guards searched out cells several times before the play, allegedly looking for weapons and escape tools, but the real intention was to rattle us. The play turned out to be one of the most peaceful evenings ever in the prison. No stabbings. No fights. No arguments. No drugs—with the exception of our spotlight operator, Troy, who got drunk on prison wine (made from yeast and fermented potatoes) and missed half of his cues. The prisoners left their beefs and rivalries in the yard and cell blocks and came together to watch a show. We worked till two in the morning under the supervision of Mr. Rathmore, tearing the set down. We were exhausted but not tired. It's the "good-tired feeling" you get when you have worked really hard at something you believe in.

The next afternoon I passed by the auditorium on my way back from recreation period in the big yard. The auditorium door was open, which was unusual. Every door and gate in Leavenworth stays locked, with a guard nearby. I entered and stood in the back of the auditorium. The stage was empty, but my mental cinema could clearly see and hear the performance and the applause from the night before. One by one, my cast and crew drifted in and stood near me quietly watching the stage. Joseph Omiwale, Willie "Subhi" Post, Ernest "Nitro" Jenkins, Mr. Cody, Death, Struck, Tito, Raphael, Abdush Shakur, Donald Lowery, and Native American leader Leonard Peltier, who was our adviser and dramaturge. Abdush broke our collective meditation. "It's true what they say," he said with a smile. "You always return to the scene of the crime."

We laughed and continued to linger in the auditorium, even though we knew we were "out of bounds" and could all be sent to the hole for being in an unauthorized area without an escort.

"When is the next play?" Omiwale asked.

"I haven't written it," I replied with a shrug, never having considered a play beyond the Black History Month extravaganza.

"So write the damn thing," Subhi said, implying that I should stop fucking around and get to work.

Over the next three years I wrote several more plays, which we mounted. I collaborated with the musicians to write songs for the productions and wrote a collection of poetry. Susan L. Taylor, the editor of *Essence* magazine, saw one of the poems and published it. I was still a prisoner, but I'd found a new kind of freedom.

17

Pain to Power

All power to the people. The phrase I learned as a fifteen-year-old Panther in training came back to me as I looked around the prison yard. "Black power to black people, white power to white people, brown power to brown people, red power to red people, yellow power to yellow people, and Panther power to the vanguard," my Panther teachers emphasized.

This recognition of power comes from a true recognition of pain and oppression. An understanding that we poor and working-class people have all been exploited and enslaved in different ways. A recognizing of the commonality of that exploitation and the necessity of coming together in order to change things. It was also acknowledging that we had internalized that oppression, manifested in doubt, self-hate, mistrust, and violence. Nowhere was that more raw or clearer than in prison. The prison authorities expected, and in many ways counted on, this internalized oppression and hatred. As long as prisoners were divided, mistrustful, and violent, the force of the prison administration could reign supreme. If prisoners unified, they could run the prison, turning those cells into classrooms, conservatories, and think tanks of progressive social change.

All power to the person. My time in Leavenworth made me realize that change begins with the individual, which ran contrary to the Marxist thinking I grew up with in the movement.

> *The individual is subordinate to the organization. The minority is subordinate to the majority. The lower level is subordinate to the higher level.* —Mao Tse-tung

I was the gung-ho example of the young movement warrior who encased his feelings of confusion, betrayal, disappointment, rage, and heartbreak in a concrete ball and buried it in a place deep inside so that it wouldn't interfere with his duties as a young revolutionary.

Now, at Leavenworth, we were sitting and standing in a circle in the big yard, sharing personal stories that could be incorporated into characters I was creating for our next play, *30 Days and a Wake Up*. When you became a "short-timer" in prison, guys would ask you how much time you had left. The answer might be "twenty-nine days and a wake-up," which meant you had twenty-nine days left to do plus the morning you woke up to be released. I was amazed at the number of prisoners who would get down to their last few days and blow their release date by catching a new case (for possession of drugs or weapons, for example), or they'd get into a beef that would wind up with them killing or being killed. This new play was going to be a character study of six convicts down to their last thirty days.

Our prison troupe had become fairly tight and open about sharing stories of some of the abuse, hardships, and mistakes in their lives. It came my time to share, and I talked about the journey of the Panther baby who grew up in the movement, then on the run, and now in jail.

"You know you're suffering from posttraumatic stress, right?" said Nitro, a super-crazy, super-talented black Vietnam veteran who had been a demolitions expert in the U.S. Marine Corps.

"I've never been in the army," I responded.

"Yeah, but you were still in a hell of a war," Nitro insisted. "Look at all the shit you were just talking about. Survivor guilt; self-medicated depression; feelings of alienation, anger, sadness, and attempted suicide."

"I never tried to kill myself," I snapped.

"Man you been trying to get yourself killed for years," Nitro said, smiling, "suicide by cop, suicide by thug, suicide by prison guard."

Later, back in the cell block, Nitro showed me the symptom list for posttraumatic stress disorder in the *Diagnostic and Statistical Manual of Mental Disorders,* a manual that we had been given as a textbook in our prison behavioral psychology class taught by the University of Kansas. Of the sixteen symptoms listed, I had twelve. The cell block started spinning with the realization that the last fifteen years had not been the fragmented episodes of a young man wrestling with beliefs and identity but rather a continuum of mind-engulfing and soul-deep pain. Like the person who can't afford medical care and learns to live with a toothache or back pain, I had ignored the forces that were tearing me apart.

Around the same time I received a box of FBI files from my lawyers in response to a motion we made under the Freedom of Information Act. These were secret files the FBI kept during the COINTELPRO activities against the Black Panther Party. Large sections of the files had been redacted or blanked out in the name of ongoing "national security," but there was enough in the files to reveal how evil, insidious, and deadly the government had been in its attempts to wipe out the party.

I cried as I read what had been done to us, realized how we were divided and manipulated and made to turn against one another. My healing began with those tears. I got on my knees and said a prayer of forgiveness—for myself, for all those I may have hurt, for all who had hurt me.

Prayer, yoga, and meditation became a part of my daily routine. I read as many books as I could on positive thinking, spirituality, and transformation. I incorporated these ideas into my theater work with my fellow prisoners and into my daily conversations with every prisoner I met. I began using the words "love" and "healing" and talked about our ability to mend ourselves behind bars and to pass the energy of transformation on to other prisoners and to our family and friends on the outside. I was still fired up about progressive social change. Racism, poverty, and oppression were real things that needed to be confronted with organized movements, but I now felt that we needed to challenge these things from a place of "progressive love" and "creative personal transformation."

The University of Kansas offered a college extension program through which professors taught nightly classes in the recreation center. Prisoners who worked hard could earn degrees with full rights and honors in psychology and sociology. I took eighteen credits a semester and earned degrees in both areas. Our professors were tough, demanding the same amount of attention, rigor, homework, and research as they did from their students on the main campus. The prison college students were terrified of these professors, especially Dr. Moro, a petite woman in her sixties. She taught English and would rip everyone's assignments to shreds. One day she came to class with passages of the Bible that she had redlined for grammatical errors. We figured that if God and Jesus were catching it, what chance did we have? We stood in the big yard after taking her final exam, shaking in fear, worried about our grade-point averages. *Power to education.*

Members of the theater group and my prison college class-mates would go back to their cell blocks or courts in the big yard and engage their friends and associates with these new ideas about progressive change and transformation. We also continued to discuss class and race and the phenomenon of prison as an industry. The United States ranked third behind the Soviet Union and South Africa in the number of people locked up in its prisons. With the dissolution of the Soviet Union and the ending of apartheid, the United States would become number one.

The prison business was lucrative. Federal prisoners worked in factories for pennies an hour, making mailbags for the post office, T-shirts for the military, furniture for federal offices, and other products that were sold for fair-market rates, creating profits in the millions. Private corporations began building and running prisons under subcontract agreements with cities and states, their real profits coming not from boarding fees but from the slave labor of the prisoners.

It is cheaper to send someone to Columbia or Harvard University than to keep them in prison. The Leavenworth theater group and the college programs dramatically reduced gang activity and violence in the big top. Statistics show that there was a significant drop in recidivism for prisoners who took college courses on the inside. Yet prison recreation and education budgets have since been cut. Many of the arts and college programs no longer exist. Surprisingly, a lot of the legislation that was passed to toughen up prisons was sponsored by some of the most liberal members of Congress. It was a way for Democratic and liberal politicians to get "I'm tough on crime" votes in the face of tough election battles with Republicans.

My life in Leavenworth didn't turn into a giant kumbaya circle of harmony when I started doing the work of transforming pain to power. I was part of a prison-administration-sanctioned organization called the African Culture Society. I spent a lot of hours refereeing disagreements with members who wanted to solve problems in the old-school style. The idea of parliamentary procedure, voting, consensus, and negotiation was new and sometimes difficult learning for guys who grew up on the street and in jail.

I would sometimes hear grapevine rumors about other prisoners who didn't like me and who thought I was getting too much attention or "play" because of all my activities. I would ignore the rumors and continue to create power by sharing the power, teaching prisoners how to run the theater company, the African Culture Society, and the tutoring work-shops without me. I felt the real point in this work was to create something that would last without me, a grassroots garden of humanity in the midst of a steel, concrete, barbed-wired jungle.

In the sixth year of my sentence an FBI agent and a federal prosecutor came to Leavenworth to see me. Dr. Mutulu Shakur, a groundbreaking acupuncturist and Black Liberation movement leader, had been arrested on a federal fugitive warrant. The Feds wanted me to testify against him in exchange for an early release. My attorney, Bill Mogulescu, was present at the meeting, and I responded with a polite but firm no. The Feds left angry and disappointed. Bill and I hung out in the visiting room, catching up and talking about one last appeal motion that I had pending before federal judge Kevin Duffy. The motion was known as Rule 35; the sentencing judge had the ability to reduce the initial sentence based on new information or mitigating circumstances.

Bill believed that we had a shot at getting my sentence reduced. He would send the judge my straight-A college transcripts from each semester along with a commendation I had received from the NAACP for organizing an event in the prison whereby prisoners donated two thousand dollars of their commissary money for African famine relief. I also had received a commendation for helping save a prisoner from a burning cell. The judge also had letters from Joyce about our young son, Jamal, who had been hospitalized a number of times because of sickle-cell anemia. I had less faith than Bill in my appeal chances, convinced that the Feds would make me do every day of my sentence.

When I got back to the cell block, a rumor about me was circulating, slithering about like a deadly serpent. Word was, a group of prisoners wanted to kill me because I had been talking to the Feds. A Jamaican prisoner I was close to named Hopeton told me to stay out of the yard so that he and his crew could take out the convicts who were threatening to kill me. I thanked Hopeton for having my back and went to the yard anyway.

Sure enough, there were two groups of black prisoners squaring off and ready to go to war. A prisoner named Mike was the one who started the rumor and the beef. He was one of the guys who seemed bothered by my high profile at Leavenworth. Mike got wind that the Feds tried to make me an offer and started the rumor that I was cooperating, an indefensible violation of the convict code.

Now other prisoners in the yard wanted to kill Mike for starting a bad rumor. I pounded my fists on one of the yard's wooden tables as I told my "allies" how insane and backward it would be for us to start killing each other over a bullshit rumor. I pointed out that this is exactly how the Feds used COINTELPRO to destroy the Panther Party. Lesson learned. Beef settled. Or so I thought.

Over the next few weeks, Mike continued to hammer at the rumor. Rudy Giuliani, who was then U.S. attorney for the Southern District of New York, wrote a letter to Judge Duffy asking him to deny my motion for sentence reduction because I had recently turned down a chance to cooperate.

Jill Soffiyah Elijah, a brilliant black female attorney, who is now a Harvard law professor, flew out to Leavenworth to bring me a copy of the letter. I handed the letter to Mike in the mess hall where he sat at a table filled with his cronies. "If you don't believe me, maybe you'll believe the Feds." Still he persisted, telling other convicts that he planned to kill me when the time was right.

Finally, one night Mike stepped into my cell with fire in his eyes. I could tell from his breathing that he was armed and that in seconds we would be in a life-and-death battle over a knife. "What do we have to do to squash this beef?" I asked Mike as we stared each other down. A guard came by. Mike unballed his fist and started to back out of the cell.

"Ain't nothin' you can do," he said. "If my mother had a terminal disease and you were the only person on the planet that could save her, that bitch would have to die."

One of my close friends at Leavenworth had been doing all he could to mediate a peace between Mike and me. He now gave me a piece of chilly but truthful advice: "Convicts feed on weakness. You won't let any of us kill this dude. If you don't kill him, then Mike or one of these other convicts is gonna kill you, just because convicts feed on weakness." College, plays, fund-raisers, healing—and here I was, still trapped by the convict code. I wasn't about to snitch on Mike to the authorities, and I wasn't going to let anyone else fight my battles for me. Instead I made two blackjack weapons out of batteries—which they let us have for our portable radios—placed in sweat socks.

I tracked Mike down in the prison law library. He saw me enter, looked at me with contempt, and went back to taking notes from a law book. I walked behind him and gripped my blackjacks hidden in the deep pockets of my prison coat. I knew from my martial arts training how and just where to strike and kill him. I began to pull the blackjacks from my pocket. Then a voice whispered in my ear, a woman's voice: "Don't do this." The voice was firm, clear, and undeniably real. It was my mother's voice, Gladys, who died when I was ten years old. I released the grips on my blackjacks and went back to my cell. I unknotted the sweat socks and let the batteries fall on the floor. I hung my head and sobbed. If I have to die in prison because I refused to live this part of the convict code, then so be it.

The next day Mike was taken to the hole, then transferred to another prison. The guards had done a routine shakedown of the cell block and found two knives stashed in his cell. Then the very next day I got the news that Judge Duffy had reduced my sentence. The commendations and the time off I received for good behavior meant that I would be released in less than two months. Had I let anger prevail and attacked Mike, I would have spent another ten to twenty years in prison. Had I not listened to the "angel's voice" and submitted to the instincts of my higher self, my sentence would have never been reduced.

Finally, fifty-eight days and a wake-up later, I watched the front gate of Leavenworth roll open. Joyce was waiting for me at the bottom of the Leavenworth steps, and I ran down to her. Before I could hug her, she handcuffed our wrists together with a pair of toy plastic cuffs, held our hands high so the guards in the tower could see, and yelled, "I sentence you to life with me." The convicts from the cell block whose windows faced the front cheered. We kissed and walked toward a car that would take us to the airport, back to where I could restart my life.

18

Making an Impact

I was released on Christmas Eve 1987, having served about half of the sentence imposed on me. Jamal Jr., who was five years old, hugged me and said that my being home was the best Christmas present. We stayed with Joyce's parents in Queens for three months while I worked to save enough money for an apartment in Harlem. I worked part-time as a paralegal for two dynamic African American attorneys, Anthony Ricco and Talif Warren. I also worked part-time sanding wood floors and painting for my friend David LeSeur.

Freedom felt like a mixed blessing. There were many Panthers still in prison doing long sentences on questionable convictions, like Sundiata Acoli and Sekou Odinga from the Panther 21 and Mumia Abu-Jamal, whose death penalty case has been taken up by Amnesty International.

The young gunslingers who sold drugs on my Harlem block didn't know what to make of me. One day in my suit (the only one I owned), the next day in dirty coveralls. I heard one of them whisper, "Five-oh," the street code for a cop, as I headed to the subway. I turned around, intent on getting things straight on the spot. I wasn't about to have a false rumor put my family in danger or get me shot in the back. I walked up to the gunslinger who was the obvious leader of the crew and said, "My name is Jamal Joseph. I want you to tell the dude who you work for to tell the dude who he works for to check with his man, who's in the penitentiary, and find out who I am." I turned and walked away. Three days later I passed the same group of gunslingers. The leader nodded respectfully and said, "How you doin', Brother Jamal?"

This time was the height of the crack epidemic. Drugs and guns were everywhere. The young drug crews had TEC-9s, Uzis, and Desert Eagle pistols. They were better armed than the Black Panther Party ever was, but they didn't have the most important and first weapon that I was given the day I walked into the Panther office: a book that dealt with life and change and mentors compelling them to read, learn, and understand the socioeconomic conditions that had brought them to this place.

One hot early July night, the dealers and gunslingers were setting off firecrackers. The popping and the explosions were so loud that they woke up Jamal and the new addition to the family, our infant son, Jad, even though our windows were closed and the air conditioner was on. I hopped out of bed and got dressed.

"Where are you going?" Joyce asked.

"To talk to these kids about these firecrackers. It's one o'clock in the morning. Old folks are trying to get some rest in this building. Working folks have to get up in a few hours and go to their jobs."

"You don't know these kids," Joyce replied. "We just moved here."

"When I grew up, any adult in the neighborhood could talk to you, and you'd listen. You had to respect your elders."

"But these kids are different, and they don't know you," Joyce said. "They don't know that you're a former Panther, that you did time, taught karate, and if they knew, they probably wouldn't give a damn."

"I'm going anyway," I said, reaching for the doorknob.

Joyce threw herself against the door and blocked my way. "You can't go," she yelled.

"Why not?" I responded.

"Because it might not be firecrackers down there. It might be guns."

I paced in front of the door. Panther in a cage. Feeling more trapped in my Harlem apartment than I did in my Leavenworth cell. "I have to do something," I declared, pleading at the same time.

Joyce grabbed a pen and paper and shoved it at me, desperately trying to calm the caged Panther down. "Then write, just write."

I sat on the hallway floor, and a poem flowed from my troubled heart to the page, all about my frustration, and the inevitability of more death on the streets of Harlem, and the urgent need to try to do something, any something that could break the cycle of fear and death.

I continued to work two, sometimes three, jobs and performed community theater on the weekends. My big break in theater came when Charles Dutton, a very talented actor who had served time in prison before attending Yale Drama School, introduced me to Voza Rivers.

Voza was the executive producer of Harlem's New Heritage Theatre, founded by Roger Furman. Voza had produced hundreds of plays and concerts, including *Sarafina!,* which was then running on Broadway. He did a staged reading of my play *30 Days and a Wake Up* at the Schomburg, costarring Charles Dutton and Joyce Walker Joseph, my wife. After that there were readings and productions of my plays around the city, and I won several awards, including a New York Foundation of the Arts Fellowship in playwriting.

A friend from the Panthers named Tony Rodgers took me to breakfast a few months after I was first released from prison. Tony was then a vice president at City College and a cofounder of Harlem Week, along with Lloyd Williams. Tony told me about a job opening at the Harlem campus of Touro College.

"Tony, I have a record," I said, doubting the job lead.

"But you have a college degree," Tony said. "University of Kansas, summa cum laude." Tony laughed and made me promise to submit my résumé.

Panther founder Bobby Seale told me that whenever he got a job, the FBI would show up the next day and scare the people who had hired him by talking about his Black Panther affiliation. I wrote up a résumé and put my Black Panther membership and time in Leavenworth under "Additional Experience." Might as well lay it all out rather than have the FBI get me fired before I even started the gig.

To my surprise, my job application and initial interview got me a second interview, this time with Stephen Adolphus, the dean of Touro's School of General Studies. He was a distinguished-looking white academic, with glasses, a vest, and a serious manner. He, of course, went right to the "Additional Experience" part of my résumé.

"Mr. Joseph, I see you spent time in prison."

"Yes, and as you can see I graduated with highest honors in psychology and sociology," I said, trying to steer him back to the good points of my résumé.

"And you were really a member of the Black Panther Party?" he pressed.

"Yes, and I was a counselor at Infinity House Drug Program and day camp director at the Settlement House," once again trying to steer him.

"So you really understand the community. If we hired you as a recruitment counselor, you could really get out there in a grassroots sort of way and find students." It turned out that Dean Adolphus had used *Soul on Ice* and *The Autobiography of Malcolm X* when he was an English professor at the State University of New York, and he pioneered prison college programs when he worked for the New York State Board of Regents.

He hired me on the spot, and I worked for Touro College for seven years as a counselor, director of student activities, and professor. Our family grew to three when Joyce gave birth to our daughter, Jindai.

I worked with Laurie Meadoff, Malik Yoba, and Kate Hillis at the City Kids Foundation, using theater arts to empower kids to create stories of personal experience, leadership, and social change. City Kids was located in Tribeca, in lower Manhattan, but it attracted teenagers from all over the city.

I began writing and directing educational films and documentaries. Michelle Satter, the director of the Sundance Film Institute, gave me a chance to spend a summer at its Utah facilities as a directing fellow. Many of the people who mentored my film have become lifelong friends, including Alice Arlen, Jim Hart, Scott Frank, and James Schamus.

In 1998, James Schamus and Lewis Cole gave me an opportunity to teach screenwriting at Columbia University. There I became part of a gifted and dedicated faculty and have had the pleasure of working with some amazing students, including Randy Dottin and Simon Kinberg, and I became the first African American chair of the Film Program in the School of the Arts.

In 1997 Andre, a sixteen-year-old man-child who grew up in our building, was killed at a party in Harlem. He confronted a young gunslinger who had disrespected his sister, and the gunslinger shot Andre.

Andre's mother supported her family as a secretary. She was mother and father to her children, teaching them to value education and hard work. When she got news of her son's death, her apartment became too small to contain her grief. She ran out to the street and wailed.

Joyce and the other women from our building surrounded her, held her, and consoled her. The men from our building stood a few feet away, watching helplessly as another black mother mourned the loss of her son. This could have been

Alabama during slavery, Mississippi after a lynching, or South Africa during apartheid—but this was Harlem. This was my home. This was now. I felt angry and impotent.

I was still in mourning from the death of my godson, Tupac Shakur, who had been killed in Las Vegas a year earlier. Tupac called me Uncle Jamal, and we had been close since he was a little boy. He visited my karate dojo when he was young and liked to spar with the biggest students in class. He would amaze us with his poems and rhymes and thoughts about life, politics, and the black struggle for liberation. By the time I returned from prison, Tupac was performing with the rap group Digital Underground and about to embark on his solo music and acting career. We would get together and talk for hours about everything, from Bruce Lee to Malcolm X.

Our ongoing battle was over "thug life," a concept and movement Tupac had started.

Essentially, thug life was a celebration of young brothers who hustled, gangbanged, and lived outside the law to survive. "Pac, Malcolm X, Huey Newton, George Jackson, and Bobby Seale were thugs who became politically aware and became leaders of the movement," I would argue. "You are a Black Panther cub who grew up in the movement; why are you headed the other way?"

"Uncle Jamal, I just got to keep it real with street soldjas who kept it real with me," Tupac would counter. "When I was on the street, trying to survive, it was the thugs who showed me love." Tupac believed his mission was to make his art speak everyone's truth, from the thugs and the welfare mothers to the heroes of the movement.

When I heard that Tupac had been shot in the lobby of Quad Recording Studio in Manhattan, I rushed to see him at Bellevue Hospital. Police, press, and fans were massed in front of the hospital; hospital security officers blocked my way in the lobby. "Let Jamal through," Gloria Jean, Tupac's aunt, yelled. "He's family." One of the smaller waiting rooms had been set up for Tupac's family and close associates. About twenty-five of us were there, standing vigil, waiting to be part of the next group of four to go to Tupac's bedside.

I was near the elevator with Tupac's mother, Afeni, and Glo about to go up to his room when the doors opened and Tupac limped off, bandaged and bloody. I grabbed a wheelchair and we sat him down. "Pac, what are you doing?"

"I don't want to stay here. They're trying to kill me."

We wheeled him into the waiting room. Afeni tried to convince him to go back to his room, but he refused. "Jamal, you talk to him," Afeni asked.

I knelt by the wheelchair and placed my forehead against Tupac's. It was a private gesture of affection we had made up when he was little. "Pac, you're wounded and you're bleeding. We will stay with you around the clock, but you need a doctor's care," I pleaded.

"I don't want to stay here, Uncle Jamal. You can take me

someplace else, but I don't want to stay here." Tupac's mind was set. Watani (Tupac's manager), Afeni, and I wrapped Tupac in a blanket and began to move him toward the door.

A black hospital security sergeant blocked our way. "He can't leave," the sergeant ordered in a Caribbean accent.

"Is he under arrest?" I asked.

"No, but he can't leave," the sergeant insisted.

I pulled the sergeant to the side. "Sir, look around you," I said calmly. "There are ten or so former Black Panthers, ten Fruit of Islam security men, and ten young street soldiers. Don't tell us we can't leave. Kindly bring us the form so Mr. Shakur can sign himself out, and I would appreciate if you would escort us to the back door so we can avoid the press and the fans." My account of those present was close enough for the sergeant to get the point. He came back with the forms, and we whisked Tupac out the back of the hospital and into a waiting car.

A few weeks later Tupac was back in Bellevue, this time in the prison ward. He had been convicted of sexual misconduct after being acquitted of more serious rape and assault charges. Tupac always maintained his innocence. He said he was asleep in a different room when other people in his entourage got involved with the young woman who had brought the charges. My paralegal ID got me through security at the hospital and into a private booth with Tupac. He was still limping from his wounds, but he looked strong. He wore a blue prison jumpsuit.

We hugged, touched foreheads, and sat down to talk. "Uncle Jamal, before you start," Tupac said in anticipation that I might continue our ongoing debate about thug life, "let me tell you a story. They brought in a nineteen-year-old brother to the prison ward from a jail upstate because he needs a hernia operation. He sees me and bugs out. 'Damn Tupac, it's you. You're my hero!' he said. I told him time out and asked why was I his hero? And he said, 'You be gettin' all the money, you be gettin' all the bitches, you be shootin' at the police!' I stepped back and thought for a moment. 'If that's why I'm your hero, then I don't need to be anybody's hero,' I told him."

Tupac said that in that moment he realized that thug life was dead. He wanted to use his fame to create youth centers around the country where kids could get free training in creative arts and leadership. Pac told me that he was done smoking weed and drinking because they had clouded his thinking and made him "act out" in ways he regretted. "I'm going to deal with my inner peace and sobriety one day at time, the way Mommy does," he said, referring to Afeni.

Tupac also told me he was going to die. "They have to kill me," he said, "because I'm a Shakur. My only choice is whether I go out like Malcolm X or like Tony Montana from *Scarface.* And I've decided I want to go out like Malcolm X." I told Tupac that he shouldn't claim an early death as inevitable, especially since he was talking about so many positive things. I had also prophesied my own warrior's death by age eighteen, and here I was brainstorming with Tupac about film, music, and theater projects as well as arts programs for the youth.

Unfortunately, Tupac's prophecy would come true eighteen months later. He was released from prison after eight months and immediately began to live and create at a velocity that is impossible to imagine. By the time he was killed, only a few months later, Tupac had recorded hundreds of songs, filmed movies and music videos, performed concerts, written essays and screenplays, created plans for his youth arts centers, and launched the One Nation project to end the dangerous feuding in hip-hop.

There was a group of teenage boys in Harlem who called themselves "25 to Life," because they believed they would be dead or in jail before they were twenty-five. It's what they saw all around them—fathers, uncles, older brothers, all going to jail or being murdered. Their negative projections were reinforced by songs, music videos, and films that showed young black men dying on the streets after trying to survive "by keeping it real." Their belief was memorialized by Tupac's life, who was killed when he was twenty-five.

I told Tupac death would not take him, yet it did, I thought weeks later as I stood with men from my building helplessly watching the women cry over the murder of young Andre.

Another senseless, violent death. Maybe there was more I could have said or done for Tupac, I thought, just as maybe there was more I could have done for Andre. I was helping to run a youth program in downtown Manhattan. What about in Harlem where I live? I thought. If Andre, or perhaps even the boy who shot him, were in a creative arts workshop instead of out partying or doing drugs on the street, then maybe Andre would be alive.

These pointless deaths had to stop. I knew I had to do something, I had to fight the battle right here in Harlem where I lived, and I knew what my weapons would be.

I went to Voza with the idea of starting a creative arts and leadership program in Harlem, knowing that the money to support it wouldn't come from the city. Mayor Giuliani had cut much of the funding for arts programs in the schools. I knew the power of arts to effect change from my experiences of Leavenworth, and more recently from working with City Kids. Voza agreed to help me, and we each took money from our own bank accounts and started IMPACT Repertory Theatre. Joyce and Alice Arlen were part of our initial founding team. Raymond Johnson and Courtney Bennett soon joined us, bringing their ideas and energy to the founding circle.

IMPACT started in the basement of Minisink Townhouse in Harlem with nine young people, including Jamal Jr., Jad, and Jindai. That was more than fourteen years ago, and since then a thousand kids have passed through the program, in the process gaining a sense of themselves as young artists and leaders through music, dance, drama, and film. Many of these young people have since gone to college and grad school and are following careers in medicine, law, education, and counseling. IMPACT alumni come back to teach and mentor current members. We started out with the idea for a program to help individuals and in the process have built a community of artistic change.

IMPACT has presented hundreds of shows at venues ranging from schools, prisons, shelters, and community centers all the way to the Apollo Theater, New York's Public Theater, and the Kennedy Center in Washington DC. Jim Hart, Richard Lewis, and Kirsten Sheridan gave IMPACT a chance to play the role of a gospel choir in the movie *August Rush*. We asked Richard, the producer, and Kirsten, the director, if we could write the song for our segment. They agreed and the song, "Raise It Up," was nominated for an Academy Award.

Although I was one of the official nominees, along with Tevin Thomas and Charles Mack, I always have contended that the nomination belonged to IMPACT. Our songs are created in a group laboratory, by a staff of young people, which for "Raise It Up" included Ray Jay, Dietrice, Antwon, Michelle, and Chapella.

And the real joy of the Academy Award nomination was standing on stage and performing the song with thirty young people from Harlem accompanied by Jamia Nash at the 2008 Oscars, telecast around the world for millions of people to see.

Bobby Seale once said when he and Huey Newton started the Black Panther Party, they carried both shotguns and law books because those were the weapons of dynamic social change. If they were starting the organization now, however, Panthers would be patrolling the streets with video cameras and laptop computers, because those are the relevant weapons of change for today.

We must continue to fight for our youth and change and, if necessary, wage that fight for change in militant and revolutionary ways. Our young people must know that they stand on the shoulders of people like Rosa Parks, Dr. King, Malcolm X, members of the Black Panther Party, and so many others. They must know that the true motivation for anything has to begin with love and that the right strategy for success includes service and dedication.

Looking back, I am proud of all that I've accomplished, all that I've done. I made mistakes along the way, but I remained true to my vision and to the tenets instilled in me by Noonie and the other positive influences in my life. I want the same for my children, who I'm proud to say are all in Ivy League schools, getting an education that will prepare them for the future.

I'm reminded of the irony of this turn of events whenever I

walk by the large statue of Alma Mater that stands in front of Low Library in the middle of the Columbia campus. She looks down at me with a look that says, "So it's Professor Joseph now, huh? I remember when you were a young Panther and all you wanted to do was burn this damn place down or die trying. Well, we both survived, and here we are. Maybe there's a future after all."

ACKNOWLEDGMENTS

Boundless thanks for the hard work and energy of Jared Hoffman, Stephanie Abou, Julian Riley, Lainie Cooke.

The support and encouragement of Joyce, Reggie Rock Bythewood, Afeni Shakur, Dhoruba Bin Wahad, Malik Yoba, James Schamus, Pastor Michael A. Walrond Jr., Carol Becker, Jana Wright, Nile Rodgers, Felipe Luciano, Kathleen Cleaver, Dr. Joseph Harris, Alice Arlen, Voza Rivers, Scott Frank, Lloyd Williams, Tony Rogers, Steve Adolphus, Jim Hart, Laurie Meadoff, William Mogulescu, Ellis Haizlip, Lewis Cole.

The family love of Jay Jr., Jindai, Jad, Elba, Luis, Miguel, Myrna, Juan Carlos, Christian, Evelyn, Claire, Bishop Snipes, Aunt Nina, nieces, nephews, grands, Roalh, Mike H., Courtney, Tevin, Charles M., Ray Jay, Dietrice, Luther, Emilia, Sekyiwa, Tony Ricco, Jamala, Glo, IMPACT, the Order of the Feather, Tapawingo, Omega Psi Phi Fraternity, Inc., Lewis Hayden no. 69, First Corinthian Baptist Church.

The sacrifice and commitment of Bullwhip, Claudia, Wonda, Mark, Kim, Brad, Diane, Brenda, Itelia, Lynn, Safiyah, Bashir, Malika, Ila, Butch, Tony, Stephanie, Sister Love, Marie, Cynthia, Brenda, Cathy, Frankie, Nicky, J. T., Omar, B. J., Yasmin, Cleo, Billy X, Vanessa, Ashanti, Gaylord, Shep, Tymon, Ronnie, Rahim, Cleo, Dee, Rosemarie, Denise Oliver, Nat Shanks.

And all the members of the Black Panther Party rank and file who were the heart of the movement.

Orphan, activist, subversive, urban guerrilla, FBI fugitive, drug addict, drug counselor, convict, writer, poet, filmmaker, father, husband, professor, youth advocate, and Oscar nominee Jamal Joseph lives with his wife and family in New York City.